W9-CSS-927

Weekend Adventures
for City-Weary
Families

Weekend Adventures

for City~Weary Families

A Guide to Overnight Trips
in Northern California

Carole Terwilliger Meyers

Other books by Carole Terwilliger Meyers:

How to Organize a Babysitting Cooperative and Get Some Free Time Away From the Kids

Eating Out With the Kids in San Francisco and the Bay Area

Getting in the Spirit, Annual Bay Area Christmas Events

Copyright © 1980 by Carole Terwilliger Meyers
All rights reserved. No part of this book may be reproduced in any form or by any means without the prior written permission of Carousel Press, excepting brief quotes used in connection with reviews written specifically for inclusion in a magazine or newspaper.

One in the series: *Weekend Adventures for City-Weary Families: A Guide to Overnight Trips in the U.S.A.*
Copyright © 1977 by Carole Terwilliger Meyers

Library of Congress Catalog Card Number: 80-24121
ISBN: 0-917120-06-X
Printed in the United States of America

first printing, December 1980

10 9 8 7 6 5 4 3 2 1

Additional copies of *Weekend Adventures for City-Weary Families* may be ordered by mail. See order form on page 195.

CAROUSEL PRESS
P.O. Box 6061
Albany, CA 94706

*in memory of Alan
and the Orient Express*

CREDITS:

Editing: Gene Meyers

Typesetting and layout: Richard Ellington

Cover design and maps: Jane Bernard

Cover illustration: Gary Thomas Kong

Printing: Braun-Brumfield, Inc.

Photos:

page 12: Roaring Camp & Big Trees Narrow-Gauge Railroad
page 14: Paul Masson
page 19: Marriott's Great America
pages 25, 27, 34, 43, 44, 45, 48, 50, 62, 73, 76, 78, 85, 91, 99, 102, 107, 128, 146, 149, 187: California Department of Parks and Recreation
page 33: Jerry Lebeck, Monterey Peninsula Visitors & Convention Bureau
page 36: Pete Amos, California Department of Parks and Recreation
page 52: Theodore Osmundson, California Department of Parks and Recreation
page 54: John Kaestner, California Department of Parks and Recreation
page 60: King Merrill Associates, Solvang Business Association
pages 63, 68, 71, 92, 94, 100, 191: Redwood Empire Association
page 65: Ansel Adams, Redwood Empire Association
page 74: Eureka Inn
pages 108, 130, 137, 142: Larry Paynter, California Department of Parks and Recreation
pages 112, 116, 189: Yosemite Park and Curry Company
page 113: John Michael Flint, Oakwood Lake
pages 118, 170: John M. Giosso, San Francisco Recreation and Park Department
page 122: Patt Gilman Public Relations
page 125: Westside & Cherry Valley Railway
page 131: 39th District Agricultural Association
page 156: Travel Systems Ltd.
pages 158, 164, 167, 168: Greater Reno Chamber of Commerce
page 162: Northstar
page 165: Boreal
page 174: Shasta-Cascade Wonderland Association
page 177: Dick Linford, ECHO
page 178: Wilderness Adventures
page 180: Shasta Llamas
page 182: Paul Herzoff, Royal Gorge Nordic Ski Resort
page 184: Bob Everson, Alpine Meadows
page 185: Vance Fox, Northstar

TABLE OF CONTENTS

Due to inflation, many of the prices quoted in this book will be out of date before the book is even published. Specific prices are mentioned only to give you an approximate idea of what to expect. Phone numbers and addresses are listed so that you may call or write to determine the current rates. All establishments listed in this book are mentioned to alert the reader to their existence; they are in no way endorsed by the author or publisher.

INTRODUCTION

It is quite frustrating to discover a town's main attractions *after* you have left. With kids in tow, parents usually don't have much time to collect and read all the brochures and books which would alert them to these facilities. This book is designed so that the reader can quickly see what items of special interest are available in the area he plans to visit. All important phone numbers and addresses necessary for obtaining further information are at the reader's fingertip. With the aid of this book, parents can more easily plan their trips and get the most out of their weekends away.

HELPFUL HINTS WHEN TRAVELING BY CAR WITH CHILDREN

Traveling anywhere in a car with children can be a trying experience for everyone concerned. Even short trips can be exhausting and leave everyone in *real need* of a vacation. Here are some suggestions on how to make a family car trip a more pleasurable experience.

- Use a luggage rack to handle the overflow from the trunk. Try to leave as much space as possible in the passenger section of the car.

- Take along blankets and pillows for napping. Towels make good covers for hot carseats and can be used in countless other ways (rolled up as a pillow, to mop up spills, etc.).

- Keep a first-aid kit in your trunk. Fill it with:

bandages	children's aspirin
antiseptic	thermometer
safety pins	scissors
tweezers	adhesive tape
a roller bandage	gauze pads
q-tips	soap
washcloth	flashlight
a few dimes for emergency phone calls	

Most of these items will fit inside a large, empty coffee can.

1

- For clean-ups pack pre-moistened towels or a damp washcloth in a plastic bag.

- Bring along a package of medium sized plastic bags. These are handy for many things. Children can use them to keep the things they collect together. They make good containers for messy items such as bibs and diapers. They come in handy to hold wet swimsuits. Etc.

- Use a shoebag, hung on the back of the front seat or on the car door, to store games and miscellaneous items.

- Pack a supply of non-messy snacks for the road. Some ideas:

fruit rolls	dried apple rings
raisins	packaged granola bars
cheese	apples
animal crackers	bananas
small cans of	small boxes of
juice, straws	dry cereal
fig newtons	

- For a long trip keep an ice chest stocked with milk, drinks, fruit, and other nutritious but perishable foods.

- Keep a good travel game book in the glove compartment.

- Bring a thermos of drinking water. Consider packing *only* water for drinks. When spilled, it isn't sticky. A fun idea is to recycle commercial plastic containers which resemble lemons and limes. Empty the citrus juice, remove the insert (an ice pick helps), rinse, and fill with water. Children can then squirt drinks into their mouths with a minimum of mess and bother. Another idea is to give each child their own thermos of water, for which they can be totally responsible.

- Bring disposable bibs. Make one by using a table napkin and an old "sweater guard" to hold the napkin around the baby's neck.

- Bring a few wrapped presents to help distract the children during their restless times. Select items which will be good additions to the goodie bag mentioned on page 6.

- Make a rest stop every few hours. This is a good time to eat, enjoy a sightseeing sidetrip, or simply stop at a playground or open field to allow the children to run off some of their pent-up energy. Roadside rest stops are spaced about an hour apart and make a good spot to refill your thermos and visit the restroom.

- Picnic when possible rather than eating in restaurants. Restaurants can be terribly confining after the already cramped experience of an automobile ride. Gas station attendants can be helpful in directing you to an appropriate park with play equipment.

- Avoid eating at drive-ins. It is usually messy to eat in the car and offers no chance to stretch, even though it does save time.

- A quick breakfast stop at a donut shop gets you on the road early and is also inexpensive.

- Buy gas in small quantities. Never fill the tank unless you are driving in desolate areas. This will require you to stop more, giving everyone a chance to stretch, get drinks, and visit the restroom.

- Adults can take turns driving. The nondriving adult can sit in the back seat with one (two, three . . .) child while the other child sits in the front with the driver. This helps keep squabbles to a minimum and also gives the back-seat parent and child a chance to spend some uninterrupted time together. And most children will jump at the chance to sit in the front seat.

- When traveling with a baby, purchase a bottle warmer which plugs into the car's cigarette lighter. You might also benefit from purchasing portable screens for the car windows. They keep the sun off baby and out of his/her eyes, and are available inexpensively at auto supply stores. Another worthwhile purchase is an inexpensive plastic cup holder which secures in the window.

- For a baby no longer on formula but still on a bottle, try placing 1/3 cup or 2 2/3 oz. of powdered milk in a baby bottle. When milk is needed, add water to make 8 oz. and shake. This eliminates the need for refrigeration and can be used on short trips or anytime you're away from home.

- Make your children navigators. Give each their own map and then let them tell you how far it is to the next town, etc. Give them each a wide felt-tip pen to trace your route as you go.

- Provide each child with a notepad to use as a trip diary. Encourage them to make entries each day. Older children can do this alone. For younger children, you can write what they dictate. Have crayons available for them to illustrate with. If you have an instant print camera, let each child take a few pictures each day to illustrate his/her diary.

- A good and inexpensive souvenir is postcards. Let your children pick a few at each destination. They could also be used to illustrate their diaries or simply held together, as a collection, with a rubber band.

- If you are going to stay where there is a pool, be sure to pack bathing caps. They are often required (even for males) and are not always reasonably-priced or easy to find on the spot.

- Plan to take along travelers' checks or cash. Surprisingly, many vacation establishments will not accept out-of-town checks or credit cards.

- Make a checklist of all the items you need to gather or buy for your trip. For instance, if you are going to the beach or river areas in the summer, you will want to consider taking along the following items:

swimsuits	sand toys
towels	inner tubes
suntan lotion	sandals/tennis shoes
beach blanket	air mattress
back rest	balls
sun umbrella	

But remember that if you do forget something, most of the places mentioned in this book are near a store where you can buy emergency replacements.

- A good item to help you get all your gear from the car to the beach is a molded plastic sled (borrowed from your winter checklist). Pack everything in the sled and drag it along the sand to your selected spot. Filled with a little water, it also makes a great place for a baby to splash and play safely.

- If you require a crib, reserve one at the time you make your room reservation. Otherwise, you may find none available when you arrive.

- Try the "mad bag/glad bag" trick. Give each child a bag filled with nickels or dimes at the beginning of the trip. Mom and/or dad begins the trip with an empty bag. Instruct them that each time they are deemed naughty, they must give up a coin to the parent's bag. If you're a liberated parent, you can let it work the other way too. Any coins left in their bag at the end of the trip are theirs to keep.

SUGGESTIONS FOR PLANNING TRIPS WITH CHILDREN

- Write or call the Chamber of Commerce or Visitors Bureau in the area you plan to visit. Ask them to send all pertinent literature. Be sure to ask for specific recommendations for families.

- Have the children help pick a destination and plan the trip. Do some research together. Look at maps. (You may want to consider joining the California State Automobile Association. It offers excellent maps and services to members.) Create a flexible agenda. Plan to allot sufficient travel time between destinations so that you can make unexpected stops along the way for exploring.

- Make advance reservations at motels and campgrounds to avoid disappointment and a frantic, last-minute search for *anything*. Reservations usually save you money as well. Inexpensive rooms tend to be reserved first, leaving the expensive (albeit usually more luxurious) rooms for last-munute arrivals. Always ask for a written confirmation. Take it along as proof of your reservation. If you must cancel, do so as soon as possible. You can usually get a complete refund if you give at least 48 hours notice.

- Take along sleeping bags for the kids. Often children will be allowed to sleep on the floor of your room at no charge. If you wish to do this, inquire ahead of time about the lodging's policy.

- Plan to start your trip early in the morning. Packing the car the night before helps. Plan to arrive at your destination early in the day to allow time to relax.

- When you arrive, reread the appropriate sections in this book to familiarize yourself with local resources and facilities. Also check the yellow pages in the telephone book for further information on things to do:

skating rinks	public swimming
horseback riding/	pools/plunges
stables	babysitting services
restaurants	bicycle rentals

Also check the local newspapers and tourist guides for current special events and activities.

THE GOODIE BAG

A good way to keep children occupied and happy on a car trip is to provide each one with their own *goodie bag.* For the bag itself you might use an old purse, a back pack, a small basket, a shopping bag, a small suitcase, a plastic bucket, or a covered metal cake pan. Whichever container you choose, be sure to have a *separate* one for each child and try to fill them with the *same* items (or equivalent items if their interests differ). A flat, hard container makes a good foundation for writing and coloring. Here are some ideas about what to put inside:

pads of paper	small scraps of
scotch tape	colored paper
colored felt pens/	gummed paper shapes
pencils	or seals
midget cars	magic slate
finger puppets	eraser
little people toys	magnetic puzzles,
story books	chess, checkers
car games	sewing cards
workbooks	magnifying glass
pencil box	photo viewer toy
blunt scissors	small chalkboard
card games	and chalk
crayons	felt board and shapes
coloring books	glue stick
pipe cleaners	etch-a-sketch toy
snap-lock plastic	sponge toys
beads	plastic bags to
paper dolls	hold collectibles

The items you choose to put in the goodie bag will depend on your child's age. Be sure to keep the bag stocked and ready to go, and keep your eyes open for new items to unveil on future trips. For younger children, be sure to bring along their *lovies*—teddy bear, blanket, etc.

I think you will find the goodie bag so useful that you will begin using it in other ways—on a rainy day, when your children are sick, when you leave them with a babysitter, and maybe even when you dine out at a restaurant!

Picnic Goodie Bag

Often I find it most convenient to just stop at a delicatessen for picnic fare. This is especially appropriate for spur-of-the-moment picnicking. To make spontaneity more convenient, I always keep in the trunk of my car a picnic blanket, a day pack (for those picnic spots that require a hike to reach), and a plastic pull-string bag stocked with paper plates, cups, napkins, plastic eating utensils, straws, a can opener, and a corkscrew.

Musical Goodie Bag

For family fun by the campfire or fireplace, pack a musical goodie bag. The following inexpensive items can be purchased in most music shops:

slide whistle	plastic flute
kazoo	whistle
small tambourine	wooden rhythm blocks
jew's-harp	ratchet
gongs	rasps
bells	harmonica
cymbals	

Beach Play Goodie Bag

Many of these items can be gathered from your kitchen. Remember to avoid glass. I prefer to store them all in one big plastic bucket and save them especially for trips to the water.

spray bottle	bucket
spatula	funnel
scoop	cooky cutters
pastry brush	strainer

plastic cups   pancake turner
measuring spoons

CONDOMINIUMS

Condominiums are a good choice for family accommodations at most resort areas, especially when the stay is for
longer than a weekend. And, though prices are not inexpensive, they are usually competitive with motels, and the condos
offer additional space in the form of separate bedrooms, living room, and kitchen. Vacation money can be stretched by
making use of the kitchen for preparing breakfast and putting
together a picnic lunch. Barbecues are often available for
cooking the evening meal. Meals out, on occasion, then become a more affordable expense.

Many condo complexes offer shared recreational facilities such as a pool, jacuzzi, and tennis courts as well as ameni-
ties such as laundry facilities and fireplaces. In the winter,
packages with nearby ski resorts are often available.

The reservation numbers listed in this book are usually
for a tenant's rental service. Because maid service and office
expenses have to be covered, the units cost more than they
would if you rented directly from an owner. If you like this
kind of lodging, be alert for advertised listings. You'll save
money that way.

GUIDELINES
FOR INTERPRETING THIS BOOK

This book is organized by geographical area. Each chapter has subsections, allowing for quick reference and detailing information which will be helpful in planning your trip. The subsections include the following:

Chamber of Commerce or Visitors Bureau: address, phone number.

Getting There: means of transportation other than a car; particularly scenic driving routes.

Special Events: annual events and where to get further information.

A Little Background: some historical and general background information about the area; what type of activities to expect.

Route: the quickest, easiest driving route; starting point is San Francisco.

Stops Along the Way: noteworthy spots to stop for snacks or sight-seeing.

Childcare: professional services or referrals. When babysitting is needed, ask your motel manager for assistance or referrals.

Where to Stay: a sampling of motels and hotels listed alphabetically and, when available, including the following information: name, address (city and zip code will always be the same as the Chamber of Commerce unless otherwise noted), phone, price for two people (often an additional charge is made for extra people—even children—and use of a crib or rollaway bed), months closed, special facilities.

Where to Camp: unusual private campgrounds.

Where to Eat: a sampling of restaurants suitable for families listed alphabetically and, when available, including the following information: name, address, phone, hours, availability of highchairs, booster seats, and children's portions. Always call to confirm any information as it frequently changes.

What to Do: activities in the area which are of interest to families. Some of these facilities are closed on major holidays. Always call first to verify hours.

Side Trips: areas of interest which are close by.

SAN LORENZO VALLEY

San Lorenzo Valley Chamber of Commerce
P.O. Box 103
Ben Lomond 95005
408/423-1631

■ *A LITTLE BACKGROUND*

Hidden in a dense redwood forest, this once popular resort area is now a little frayed around the edges. Motels and cabins, mostly relics from a heyday that is long past, are generally far from luxurious. Still, the abundance of trees, trails, and swimming holes as well as reasonable prices make this area a choice destination for families.

■ *ROUTE*

Located approximately 70 miles south of San Francisco. Take Hwy 280 to Hwy 84 to Hwy 35 to Hwy 9.

■ *WHERE TO STAY*

Ben Lomond Hylton Motel, *9733 Hwy 9, Ben Lomond 95005, 408/336-5643; $26–$30; pool, on the river.*

Griffin's Resort Motel, *5250 Hwy 9 South, Felton 95015, 408/335-4412; $18–$34; open May–Sept; cabins, playground, paddleboats, on the river; some kitchens, fireplaces, and TV.*

Jaye's Timberlane Resort, *8705 Hwy 9 South, Ben Lomond 95005, 408/336-5479; $24–$32; cottages, pool, TV, some fireplaces, two night minimum on weekends.*

Merrybrook Lodge, *Big Basin Rd. (P.O. Box 845), Boulder Creek 95006, 408/338-6813; $22–$32; open May–Oct; on the river; some cottages, kitchens, fireplaces, and TV.*

■ *WHERE TO EAT*

Scopazzi's, *Big Basin Rd., Boulder Creek, 408/338-4444; W–Sat 11:30am– 3pm, 5–11pm, Sun from 1:30pm, closed M & Tu; highchairs, booster seats, children's portions; reservations suggested.* Fine Italian food is served in the casual atmosphere of this spacious old building which dates back to 1904. Choose from entrees such as sweetbreads, veal scaloppine, fried prawns, chicken cacciatore, and prime rib. Unusual a la carte items such as chicken sauté with fresh apples and bananas, scallops sauté Bordelaise, and lamb chops sauté Toscana are available as well as a wide variety of pastas.

■ *WHAT TO DO*

Ben Lomond County Park, *on Mill Street in Ben Lomond, 408/336-9962; open daily in summer; free.* A sandy beach and rope swing accent the good river swimming. Lifeguards are on duty from noon to 6pm. A

basketball court and shaded picnic tables with barbecue facilities are
available.

Boulder Creek Park, *on Middleton Ave. east of Hwy 9 in Boulder Creek.*
A swimming hole with both shallow and deep areas is accented by a
sandy beach. Picnic tables and barbecue facilities are located in a
shady area.

Covered Bridge, *Felton.* Located at the end of a dirt road, this creaky
old bridge can still be walked on and is a choice site for picture-taking.

Highlands County Park, *8500 Hwy 9, Ben Lomond, 408/336-8551; weekend parking $1, pool: adults 75¢, 15 and under 50¢.* Located on an
old estate, this relatively new park features a pool, playground, picnic
tables, and nature trail leading to the river.

Loch Lomond County Recreation Area, *on Zayante Rd. 8 miles north
of Felton, 408/335-7424; open Mar–Oct, F–Tu 6am–sundown,
closed W & Th; $2/car.* Fishing, boating (rentals are available at $8–
$14/half day), picnicking (barbecue facilities are available) are the
main activities here. Swimming is not permitted.

Roaring Camp and Big Trees Narrow Gauge Railroad, *Graham Hill Rd.
at Roaring Camp Rd. in Felton, 408/335-4484; train operates daily
11am–4pm; adults $6.75, 3–11 $4.50, under 3 free.* This six-mile,
hour-long train ride winds through virgin redwoods and crosses over
several spectacular trestles. A stop is made at Bear Mountain, where
you may disembark for a picnic or hike and then return on a later
train. An outdoor chuckwagon barbecue restaurant operates near
the depot. Bring tidbits for the hungry ducks in the lake. And don't
forget light wraps. Though this area enjoys basically warm to hot
weather in the summer, it can get chilly on the train ride.

LOS GATOS

Los Gatos Chamber of Commerce
5 Montebello Way
Los Gatos 95030
408/354-9300

■ *SPECIAL EVENTS*

Paul Masson American Classic Chess Championships, *P.O. Box 97, Saratoga 95070, 408/257-7800; $35 entry fee.* Each summer chess enthusiasts match talents at this largest of outdoor chess tournaments in the world. In the shade of tall redwoods at the historic Paul Masson vineyards, competitors concentrate on their games, taking breaks on occasion to taste wines or attend a special seminar or demonstration. The tournament offers $21,500 in prizes and is open to all ages. The youngest entrant so far was seven. The youngest winner won in 1979 at age 19.

■ *A LITTLE BACKGROUND*

Tucked in the lush, green Santa Cruz mountains, Los Gatos is a quiet sleepy town that's beginning to wake up. It is well known for its many antique shops.

■ *ROUTE*

Located approximately 60 miles south of San Francisco. Take Hwy 101 to Hwy 17 to the Los Gatos exit.

■ *WHERE TO STAY*

Los Gatos Garden Inn, *46 E. Main St., 408/354-6446; $26–$37; pool, TV, continental breakfast included, some kitchens.* Quiet rooms in rustic Spanish bungalows are located just two blocks from Old Town.

Los Gatos Lodge, *50 Saratoga Ave., 408/354-3300; $42; cribs, pool, dining facilities.* This modern motel is located on a picturesque seven acre lot.

Los Gatos Motor Inn, *55 Saratoga Ave., 408/356-9191; $28–36; cribs, pool, color TV.*

■ *WHERE TO CAMP*

Saratoga Springs, *22801 Big Basin Way (P.O. Box 157), Saratoga 95070, 408/867-3016; $8 camping fee; day use: adults $2.50, 6–12 $1.75, under 6 free; daily June–Sept.* Facilities include a pool, barbecues, playground, game area, and hiking trails.

■ *WHERE TO EAT*

The Antique, *in Old Town, 408/354-1122; daily from 11am; highchairs, booster seats, children's portions.* The specialty here is Chicago-style pizza—made with a thick crust and topped with meat or cheese, chopped tomatoes, and plenty of oregano. A pizza for two has enough left over to serve one young child. Because the pizza requires almost half an hour to cook, consider ordering one of the huge salads or fancy drinks to help while away the time. The menu also includes regular dinners of veal, chicken, steak, and barbecued ribs, as well as hamburgers and sandwiches.

Mimi's, *in Old Town, 408/354-5511; Tu–Sun 10am–5pm, closed M; highchairs and booster seats.* Anytime is a good time to dine outside among the hanging geraniums at Mimi's, but my favorite time is at breakfast when apple pancakes and strawberry waffles are served along with more traditional fare. Exotic coffees, ice cream sundaes, and rich pastries are menu specialties.

Mountain Charley's, *15 N. Santa Cruz, 408/354-2510; Sun brunch 10am–2pm, 4–9:30pm, M–Sat 5:30–9:30pm; children's portions.* The live band, long communal tables, and young clientele add up to a lively experience in the jumping gigantic saloon. The restaurant is dark and noisy with huge wooden booths assuring privacy. Fish and prime ribs are the mainstays of the menu; children get a choice of chicken or hamburger.

Noodle Palace, *140 N. Santa Cruz Ave., 408/354-0555; M–F 11:30am–2:30pm, 5–10pm, Sat 5–10pm, Sun from 4pm; highchairs, booster seats, children's portions.* The huge dining area in this barn-like building is filled with antiques. Diners have a choice of seven spaghetti sauces served with oodles of noodles. There is also ravioli, baked chicken, and roast beef. Dinners include a salad, hot bread, beverage, and dessert.

■ **WHAT TO DO IN TOWN**

California Actors Theatre, *in Old Town, 408/354-6057.* Call for the current schedule of children's theater productions.

Jerome's, *413-A N. Monterey Ave., 408/354-6674.* Get your kids' hair cut by Jerome. He specializes in children's haircuts and entertains his young patrons with a closed-circuit TV and other flashy, interesting distractions.

Los Gatos Museum, 4 Tait St., *408/354-2646; M–Sat 1–5pm, Sun 2–4 pm; free.* Housed in a Spanish-style building, this small museum features exhibits on local history, science, and contemporary fine arts.

Novitiate Winery, *300 College Ave., 408/354-6471; tasting room: M–Sat 9am–4pm, closed Sun, tours: M–F 1:30 & 2:30pm, Sat 10 & 11am.* Jesuit cellarmasters hand-cultivate the grape harvest at this renowned winery. Part of the harvest is still used to make sacramental wine. A picnic area is available.

Oak Meadow Park, *off Blossom Hill Rd.* This 12-acre park has picnic areas, baseball diamonds, grassy fields, hiking trails, and a well-equipped playground with a *real* fire engine and airplane to climb on.

Billy Jones Wildcat Railroad, *P.O. Box 869, 408/395-9775; daily in summer 11am-5:30pm, weekends spring-fall, closed Oct-Apr; 50¢, under 2 free.* This miniature replica of a steam locomotive chugs along Los Gatos Creek for a 15-minute ride through Oak Meadow and Vasona Parks.

Old Town, *50 University Ave., 408/354-5432; daily 10am–6pm, Fri to 9pm.* Once the town elementary school, this attractive complex known as "Old Town" is now a series of interesting shops and restaurants. Each Sunday during the summer there is a free concert from noon to 3pm in the outdoor amphitheatre.

Vasona Park, *off Blossom Hill Rd.* This 175-acre park is dominated by a huge reservoir where you can rent canoes and sailboats by the hour (daily 10am–8pm, $3/hour), fish, and feed the hungry ducks and seagulls. There is also a playground, barbecue facilities, and a snack concession.

■ **WHAT TO DO NEARBY**

Garrod Farms Riding Stables, *22600 Mt. Eden Rd., Saratoga 95070, 408/867-9527; daily 8:30am–5pm; $8/hour.* Call ahead if you would like to arrange for riding lessons.

Hakone Gardens, *2100 Big Basin Way, Saratoga 95070, 408/867-2130; daily 10am–5pm; free.* Patterned after seventeenth century Zen gardens, this Japanese garden even has a tea house.

Marriott's Great America, *P.O. Box 1776, Santa Clara 95052, 408/988-1776; Sun–Th 10am–8pm, F & Sat 10am–9pm; adults $10.95, 4–11 $9.95, under 4 free.* There's no question about it—the thrill rides here are spectacular. The Willard's Whizzer, Tidal Wave, and Demon roller coasters are good, shocking fun. Though there are also plenty of kiddie rides, parents can't go on the kiddie rides and kiddies can't go on the thrill rides. Because of the high admission price (do keep in mind, though, that all rides and entertainment are free once you are inside), I recommend saving Great America to enjoy with children age 7 and over. Even some 7-year-olds won't want to go on the roller coasters, but at least they are old enough to be left to wait while their more daring parents indulge their masochistic instincts. And if you are a family with teenagers, this is THE PLACE to take them.

Villa Montalvo, *Montalvo Rd./Los Gatos-Saratoga Rd. (P.O. Box 158), Saratoga 95070, 408/867-3421; arboretum: daily 8am–5pm, free; gallery: Tu–Sun 1:30–4:30pm, closed M, 25¢.* This majestic Mediterranean-style estate was once the summer home of U.S. Senator James Phelan. Now it is the county center for fine arts and also serves as a bird sanctuary. Nature trails wind through the 175-acre estate gardens; a guide is available at the entry station. Various theatrical events are staged in the natural outdoor amphitheater and Carriage House Theater; call 408/249-8330 for information.

COAST SOUTH

SANTA CRUZ

Santa Cruz County Convention & Visitor's Bureau
P.O. Box 921
(Center/Church Sts.)
Santa Cruz 95061
408/423-6927, 423-6931
Free brochures: tree-sea tour, U.C. campus tour map,
Natural Bridges tide pools guide, four historic walking
tours.

- **A LITTLE BACKGROUND**
Santa Cruz has long been a popular summer beach resort and
is close enough to San Francisco to consider visiting for just
the day. The weather is reliably clear and sunny, and the
beach itself features fine sand and a gentle surf.

- **ROUTE**
Located approximately 80 miles south of San Francisco. Take
Hwy 101 to Hwy 17.

- **CHILDCARE**
Santa Cruz Babysitting Service, 408/476-7757.

■ *WHERE TO STAY*

Casa Blanca Motel, *101 Main St., 95060, 408/423-1570; $25–$50; ocean views, color TV, dining facilities, cribs; some private balconies, fireplaces, and kitchens; across the street from the beach.* Spacious rooms are all a little different in this converted 1918 mansion. Modern rooms are available in the 1950s annex. Continental dinners are served in the adjoining restaurant which features a "Bogie Burger" for children.

Dream Inn, *175 W. Cliff Dr., 408/426-4330; $51; color TV, pool, ocean views, balconies, dining facilities; on the beach.*

Lanai Motor Lodge, *550 2nd St., 408/426-3626; $16 and up; color TV, pool, kitchens, ocean views, private sundecks; 1 block to beach.*

Ocean Echo, *401 Johans Beach Dr., 408/475-8381; $22 and up; TV, kitchens; on the beach.* These cottages are located on a private beach.

Sea & Sand Motel, *201 W. Cliff Dr., 408/427-3400; $36–$52; TV, dining facilities, ocean views; 1 block to beach.*

U.C. Santa Cruz, *1156 High St., 95064, 408/429-2611; $18.* Five suites are available year-round. Each has a private bath and accommodates up to three people. For an additional fee you may enjoy your meals in the campus cafeteria.

West Wind Motel, *204 2nd St., 408/426-7878; $23 and up; color TV, pool, steam baths in rooms, continental breakfast included, some kitchens; across the street from beach.*

■ *VACATION RENTALS*

in homes, apartments, condominiums.

IN TOWN:

Beach Rentals, *P.O. Box 2485, 95063, 408/426-3796; $200–$300/week.*
Real Estate Center of Santa Cruz, *129 Water St., 408/426-5533.*

NEARBY:

Pajaro Dunes, *2661 Beach Rd., Watsonville, 408/722-9201, 722-4671; ocean swimming, 17 tennis courts, bicycles, paddle boats, two night minimum.*

■ *WHERE TO EAT*

Cooper House Restaurant, *110 Cooper St., 408/426-7011; daily 11:30am–9pm; highchairs and booster seats.* Enjoying a meal on the patio here is a pleasant way to spend a sunny afternoon. Live music, fresh air, happy people, and good food (soups, salads, fresh seafood) make the experience memorable.

The Crepe Place, *2027 N. Pacific Ave., 408/425-9866; Sun–Th 11am-1am, F & Sat until 3am; highchairs, booster seats.* Choose from almost a million varieties of dessert and main-course crepes.

The Crow's Nest, *2218 E. Cliff Dr., 408/476-4560; daily 11:30am–2am.* Dine outdoors, protected by a glass windbreaker, and watch the yachts come and go in the marina. Steak, hamburgers, seafood, and a salad bar are available.

The Ice Cream Bank, *1515 Pacific Ave., 408/427-0709; daily 9am–5pm.* Located in the renovated Peoples Bank Building, circa 1910, this ice cream parlor serves such unusual items as the Tasty Teller, Safe Combination, and Pay Mint.

La Fogata, *1344 Pacific Ave., 408/425-7575; W–M 10am–9pm, closed Tu.* Located in the old Palomar Hotel (now the St. George), this tasteful restaurant serves inexpensive, well-prepared, and authentic Mexican food. Unusual items are the crisp flautas, pozole (pork and hominy stew), menudo (tripe soup), and carne asada (barbecued beef). Children may enjoy the sopes (little tortillas shaped like boats and filled with tasty ground beef).

Old Santa Cruz Railway, *123 Washington St., 408/425-0525 (menu), 425-0626 (reservations); M–Th 5–9pm, F 5–10pm, Sat 4–10pm, Sun noon–9pm; highchairs, booster seats, children's portions.* Here you can enjoy "family-style dining which is reminiscent of going to Grandma's house for Sunday dinner" as well as an inexpensive fixed-price meal in which everything from soup to dessert is included. Except drinks; they are extra. Children are weighed in at the door and charged according to their weight.

Tampico Kitchen, *822 Pacific Ave., 408/423-2241; daily 9am–11pm; highchairs and booster seats.* Tasty Mexican food is served here in an ordinary cafe-style atmosphere. Especially noteworthy are the nachos (tortilla chips smothered with cheddar cheese, chiles, and onions).

"Fast Food Row." Just take a drive down Ocean Ave.

■ WHAT TO DO

Beach & Boardwalk, *Riverside Ave./Beach St. (P.O. Box 625), 408/423-5590; daily in summer 11am–10pm, weekends rest of year 11am–5pm; rides 30¢–50¢, all day ticket available.* Fortunately for families, this is one boardwalk which has not degenerated over the years. The mile-long arcade follows the beach and passes thrill rides which include the rickety old wooden "Giant Dipper" roller coaster and a refreshing flume water ride "Logger's Revenge." An old-fashioned merry-go-round, built in New Jersey in 1911 and one of only four remaining classic carousels in California, features 62 horses, a 342-pipe organ, brass rings, and free rides for parents who wish to stand with their little ones.

Lighthouse Point, *on W. Cliff Dr.; weekend afternoons; free.* Seal Rock, home to a herd of sea lions, is visible off shore from this quaint lighthouse. From Steamer Lane you can get an excellent view of the surfers.

Mission Santa Cruz, *126 High St., 408/426-5686; daily 9am–5pm; donation.* Built in 1794, the original mission was destroyed by fire in 1856. This replica was built nearby the original mission site and houses a small museum.

Municipal Wharf, *near the Boardwalk.* Stroll down the pier and watch the surfers and fishermen angling from the side. Deep sea fishing trips originate here. If you're hungry, you might want to stop at **Malio's Seafood Restaurant** for a fresh seafood dinner.

Mystery Spot, *1953 Branciforte Dr. (2½ miles north of town), 408/423-8897; daily 9:30am–5pm; adults $2, 5–11 $1, under 5 free.* Gravitational forces appear to be defied in this relatively small spot (150 ft. diameter) located in the redwoods.

Natural Bridges State Beach, *on W. Cliff Dr., 408/423-4609; $2/car.* While you picnic and sun on the sandy beach, you can marvel at the unusual sandstone arches and rock formations which have been pounded out here by the surf. This is a good spot for swimming and exploring tide pools. From October to February great numbers of Monarch butterflies make their homes here.

Pacific Garden Mall, *Pacific Ave. between Water & Cathcart Sts.* Take a walk down the five landscaped blocks of Pacific Avenue in downtown Santa Cruz. There are many conventional stores in the parklike setting as well as boutiques, art galleries, and cafes. The courthouse, circa 1895, is known as the Cooper House and has been converted into a mini-shopping complex.

Santa Cruz Museum, *1305 E. Cliff Dr., 408/429-3773; Tu–Sat 10am–5pm, closed Sun & M; free.* Located across the street from a fine beach, this museum displays Indian relics and costumes as well as an unusual collection of sea shells.

Small Craft Harbor, *2200 E. Cliff Dr.* Bring a picnic lunch or pick up supplies at the deli located in the shopping area near the parking lot. Relax and enjoy watching the ships sail in and out of the harbor while you sunbathe on the beach. Seals can often be observed frolicking close to shore.

University of California, Santa Cruz Campus, *1156 High St., 95064, 408/429-0111.* Three walking tours are available to acquaint you with this scenic U.C. campus. Self-guided tour maps are available on the campus. A free shuttle bus loops the grounds during the school year but does not run during the summer. If you get hungry, try the **Whole Earth Restaurant**; it is open to the public and serves organic vegetarian food.

CAPITOLA

Capitola Chamber of Commerce
c/o The Craft Gallery
115 Capitola Ave.
Capitola 95010
408/475-6522

■ *SPECIAL EVENTS*
For information on the annual sand sculpture contest, arts and
crafts fair, and floating parade of flower-covered boats down
Soquel Creek—all of which occur during the September Begonia Festival—contact: Begonia Festival, P.O. Box 501.

■ *A LITTLE BACKGROUND*
This historic beach resort dates back to the 1800s. Now it is
basically an artsy-craftsy beach town. The lovely beach offers
swimming in the calm ocean waters or wading in the fresh
water of Soquel Creek. Be cautious, however, as sometimes
the water isn't so fresh.

■ *ROUTE*
Located approximately five miles south of Santa Cruz on Hwy 1.

■ *WHERE TO STAY*
Capitola Inn, *820 Bay Ave., 408/462-3004; $42 and up; kitchens, color
TV, pool, free bus service to beach.*
Raynal's Harbor Lights Motel, *5000 Cliff Dr., 408/476-0505; $44; cribs,
ocean views, private balconies, TV, kitchens; across from the beach.*
Venetian Court Motel, *1500 Wharf Rd., 408/476-6471; $34.50–$44.50;
some ocean views and fireplaces; on the beach.* Some overnight rentals are available in this mini-village of charming pastel stucco units,
but in the summer most lodgers grab them up for at least one week.

■ *VACATION RENTALS*
IN TOWN:
For information on beach front summer house rentals call 408/338-
6291. Call by October for the following summer. $250–$275/week.
NEARBY:
Aptos Seascape, *#1 Seascape Blvd., Aptos, 408/688-6941; $37.10 and
up; golf course, tennis courts, lodge; townhouses on the beach.*

■ *WHERE TO EAT IN TOWN*

Mimi's Ice Cream Cart. Be on the lookout for pretty Mimi pedaling her ice cream bike. She sells cold ice cream to hot and hungry tourists.

Shadowbrook, *1750 Wharf Rd., 408/475-1511; M–F 5–10pm, Sat 4–11 pm, Sun 2–9pm; highchairs, booster seats, children's portions.* Located on the banks of Soquel Creek, diners reach this lovely restaurant by riding a bright red, self-operated cable car down the flower-laden hill from the street above. Specialties are prime rib and abalone. For dessert a special treat is the crepe patissiere (a thin crepe filled with a custard and topped with caramel sauce).

■ *WHERE TO EAT NEARBY*

The Carrousel Ice Cream Parlor, *2120 Soquel Ave., 408/429-1560; daily 11am–11pm.* This is a great destination for a quick snack of ice cream, hot dogs, or candy.

Charles Dickens Restaurant, *9051 Soquel Dr., Aptos, 408/688-7800; M–Sat 11am–2:30pm, 5:30–9:30pm, closed Sun; highchairs, booster seats, children's portions.* Though you won't find porridge served in this rustic building, you will find homemade soups, salads, sandwiches, hamburgers, omelettes, and last but not least—avocado pie. Dinner sees a switch to a continental menu.

Greenhouse Restaurant at the Farm, *5555 Soquel Dr., Soquel 95073, 408/476-5613; M–Sat 11:30am–4pm, 5–10pm, Sunday brunch 9am–2pm, 5–10pm; booster seats; reservations suggested.* Dine in the beautiful garden greenhouse or in the Victorian front room of this real farmhouse located on a working farm. Omelettes, quiches, hamburgers, fresh fish, steaks, and homemade soups—all including access to a salad bar—are among the varied items offered on the menu. Also on the farm are an antique shop, a nursery, and a produce stand selling the farm's own freshly grown produce.

■ *WHAT TO DO*

Antonelli Begonia Gardens, *2545 Capitola Rd., 408/475-5222; daily 9am–4:30pm.* Acres of indoor plants, ferns, and beautiful begonia baskets can be viewed and purchased here. Peak of bloom is August and September.

Bargetto Winery, *3535-A Main, Soquel, 408/475-2258; daily 10am–5:30pm.* Enjoy samples from this winery at their outdoor tasting bar.

Cornucopia, *209 Capitola Ave., 408/475-2844.* Tucked away in the back of another store, this is where you go to buy suntan lotion scented with essence of watermelon, coconut, almond, or musk.

Shaffer's Tropical Gardens, *1220 41st Ave., 408/475-3100.* Here you can walk through rooms filled with orchids and other unusual indoor plants.

MONTEREY PENINSULA

■ *A LITTLE BACKGROUND*

The Monterey Peninsula is well-established as a tourist retreat. Popular for years because of its proximity to San Francisco, the area offers all types of overnight accommodations. Dining here is an adventure; part of the fun is discovering your own favorites and then returning to them each time you visit. Formerly the off-season was the entire winter. Now, due to the area's immense popularity, there is no off-season. It is essential that you have reservations for lodging as well as for most of the more popular restaurants.

■ *ROUTE*

Located approximately 125 miles south of San Francisco. Take Hwy 101 to Hwy 17 to Hwy 1.

■ *STOPS ALONG THE WAY*

The Giant Artichoke, *Hwy 1, Castroville, 408/633-3204.* Located in "the artichoke capital of the world," this novelty restaurant makes

a good rest stop. You may purchase picnic supplies or snack on artichoke specialties such as French fried artichokes dipped in mayon-
naise, artichoke soup, artichoke nut cake, and steamed artichokes.
Other more standard short-order items are available as well.

MONTEREY

Monterey Peninsula Visitors &
Convention Bureau
P.O. Box 1770
(380 Alvarado St.)
Monterey 93940
408/649-3200

■ *SPECIAL EVENTS*

Bing Crosby Golf Tournament, *in Pebble Beach, January.* Contact
Visitors Bureau for details.

Adobe House Tour, *April.* Contact Visitors Bureau for details.

Laguna Seca Races, *Triple Crown in May, Historic Auto Races in August, Grand Prix in October.* Write: P.O. Box 2078, Monterey 93940.

Jazz Festival, *September.* Write: P.O. Box Jazz, Monterey 93940,
408/373-1219.

Concours d'Elegance *(showing of classic vintage and antique cars), August.* Write: United Way, P.O. Box 1926, Monterey 93940.

■ *WHERE TO STAY*

Casa Munras Garden Hotel, *700 Munras Ave. (P.O. Box 1351), 408/375-
2411; $48–$56; TV, pool, cribs, dining facilities, some fireplaces.* The
grounds here are spacious, attractive, and peaceful.

Holiday Inn, *2600 Sand Dunes Dr. (P.O. Box 710), 408/394-3321, toll-
free reservations 800/238-8000; $63.50–$73; color TV, pool, dining
facilities, cribs.* Spectacular views of the Monterey Bay may be enjoyed from the higher-priced rooms. The hotel is located outside of
town and is right on the beach.

La Fonda, *755 Abrego, 408/372-7551; $36; cribs, TV, pool, room serv-
ice, dining facilities.*

Motel Row. Modern motel accommodations abound on Munras Ave.

■ *WHERE TO CAMP*

Veterans Memorial Park, *408/646-3865, 372-8121; $5/night.* Located
in a pine forest in a city park, this campground does not accept reservations. In the summer it is usually filled by 6pm, so plan to arrive
early in the day.

■ *WHERE TO EAT*

Capone's Warehouse, *Cannery Row, 408/375-1921; M–F 4:30pm–midnight, Sat & Sun from noon; highchairs.* You enter this pizza parlor through a prohibition-era false phone booth door. Silent movies are often shown and are great for restless kiddies. Beware: pictures of risqué naked ladies line the walls; one prompted a loudly-asked sex question from my young son. The menu features Italian items such as ravioli, lasagne, fettucini, five kinds of spaghetti, as well as delicious pizza. Patrons are served at tables painted to resemble roulette tables.

The Clock Garden, *565 Abrego St., 408/375-6100; daily 11:30am–2pm, 5–10pm, Sunday brunch 10:30am–2pm; booster seats.* Located inside an historic adobe, this restaurant enjoys a reputation for fine home cooking of quality food. In my opinion the outdoor garden, with freshly potted flowers adorning every table, is the most desirable spot to dine. Brunch is casual and the best time to bring children. Reservations are not taken for brunch, so be sure to be there when they open or expect to wait. Specialties are delicious hot muffins, served with orange marmalade in a scooped-out orange shell, and frothy Ramos Fizzes. If you appreciate antique clocks, be sure to see the collection inside before you leave.

Consuelo's Mexican Restaurant, *361 Lighthouse Ave., 408/372-8111; daily 11:30am–9:30pm; highchairs, booster seats; reservations suggested.* Situated in a lovely old Victorian house complete with velvet-flocked wallpaper, Consuelo's would more appropriately be located in an adobe. The various rooms of the house have been turned into semi-private dining areas; guests may enjoy a different room each time they dine here. The menu offers typical Mexican fare along with some more unusual items. My own favorite is the flauta, made with shredded beef rolled in a delicious flour tortilla and then fried to a crisp and topped with guacamole. Appetizers come with all dinners: *hot* carrots and peppers and a crisp quesadilla served elegantly on a footed tray.

Mike's Seafood, *25 Fisherman's Wharf, 408/372-6153; daily 10am–10pm; highchairs, booster seats, children's portions.* Arrive early to take advantage of the lovely views afforded from the tables of this busy and popular seafood restaurant. Steaks, hamburgers, and chicken are also available for non-fish enthusiasts.

The Outrigger, *700 Cannery Row, 408/372-8543; daily 11:30am–2:30pm (special fixed-price buffet), 5–10:30pm; highchairs, booster seats, children's portions; reservations suggested.* Polynesian specialties, steak, and seafood are served in the dark, noisy dining room featuring spectacular views of Monterey Bay. Parents may enjoy delicious, potent tropical drinks while the kids feast on the unusual tropical desserts. The *puu puus* (appetizers)—careful with this one parents—

are delicious. Special items include a variety of curries and a Mongolian fire pot dinner. Before leaving, take the kids to see the lovely fish pond located at the back of the bar.

The Poppy, *444 Alvarado, 408/372-1336; daily 6am–midnight; highchairs and booster seats.* This is a good place to stop for a quick, reasonably priced coffeeshop meal.

Sancho Panza, *590 Calle Principale, 408/375-0095; M–Th 11am–2pm, 5–9pm, Fri & Sat 11am–9pm, Sun noon–9pm; highchairs and booster seats.* Once inside you can see why this claims to be the funkiest Mexican restaurant in town. The patio is decorated with weathered hatch covers and timbers salvaged from Cannery Row's old sardine boats. The history of the building is described as ". . . a Mexican country inn . . . located in a historic adobe built in 1841 . . . by a young Mexican for his bride." Fifteen children were raised here by that bride! The adobe was built when Monterey was still part of Mexico and is now protected by the State of California. My favorite items here are the chispa (cheeses and sauce on a flour tortilla), tostada (too much for me to eat in one sitting), guacamole, and hot chocolate flavored with cinnamon and crushed almonds. Freshly cooked tortilla chips and salsa accompany each meal.

Sardine Factory, *701 Wave St., 408/373-3775; M–Sat 11:30am–2:30pm, 5–11pm, Sun 2–10pm; highchairs, booster seats, children's portions; reservations essential.* The award-winning Sardine Factory is not a factory at all but an elegant, dimly-lit restaurant offering fresh seafood and continental gourmet items. The elegant decor is especially interesting when you realize that the building originally housed a restaurant patronized by cannery workers. All dinners are accompanied by a plate of antipasta, cheese bread, and salad presented with *chilled* forks. Come here when your kids are acting well-behaved and willing to dress in their finest—otherwise you won't be able to enjoy this very special (and expensive) dining experience.

Viennese Pastry and Coffee Shop, *469 Alvarado, 408/375-4789; M–Sat 7am–6pm, Sun 10am–4pm; highchairs, booster seats.* Local residents come here for the superb pastries (including a Viennese sacher torte) to down with a cup of coffee or tea. Breakfast and lunch items are also available.

■ *WHAT TO DO*

California Heritage Guides, *10 Custom House Plaza, 408/373-6454; adults $2, 12–17 $1, under 12 free.* The guided walking tours through Monterey's historic areas last about 1½ hours. Other tours are also available.

Cannery Row. Once an area of booming sardine canneries, Cannery Row became a ghost town when, in 1945, the sardines mysteriously disappeared from the ocean. Now this mile-long road houses restaurants, art galleries, and shops. To get in the mood, you might want to read John Steinbeck's *Cannery Row*. The Lee Chong's Heavenly Flower Grocery in Steinbeck's book is now the **Old General Store** (#835), La Ida Cafe is now **Kalisa's Cosmopolitan Gourmet Restaurant** (#851), and Doc's lab is now a private club (#800).

Edgewater Packing Company, *640 Wave St., 408/649-1899; open daily, restaurant: 6:30am–11pm, shops and carousel: noon–10pm.* This family entertainment center has a candy shop stocked with cotton candy, candy apples, and popcorn, a game room with antique and new pinball machines (the teenagers will love it), a toy store which children and limber adults can enter by crawling through a kitten's mouth, and a carousel complete with a keystone cop look-alike taking tickets. The restaurant resembles an old-fashioned ice cream parlor and serves up Oscar Hossenfellder's "fabulous formula" ice cream as well as breakfast and lunch items. There is a special children's menu offering all their favorite things (baby bottles are warmed and cheeks pinched at no charge).

El Estero Park, *Del Monte Ave./Camino El Estero/Fremont Blvd.* This park has hiking and bike trails and a lake filled with hungry ducks. Paddle boats and canoes may be rented ($4.50/hour, daily 10am–5:30pm). Children may fish from the boats. A very special playground is located by the lake on Pearl St. **Dennis the Menace Playground** (daily 10am–dusk) features equipment designed by Hank Ketchum, creator of Dennis the Menace, when he lived in the area. The unusual fun includes a hedge maze and suspension bridge. There are also picnic tables and a concession stand.

Fisherman's Wharf. Most days an organ grinder greets visitors at the wharf entrance. His friendly monkey is most anxious to take coins from the hands of children. Also, look for the freeloading sea lion who lives around the wharf pilings. Especially packaged fish is available for him at some of the bait shops. If you feed him, he'll put on a show for you. The wharf is lined with restaurants to dine in and shops to browse in. At the end, you can take a ride in a diving bell and plunge 30 ft. under the water for a fish's-eye view of Monterey Bay.

Sam's Fishing Fleet, *408/372-0577; reservations necessary.* Treat yourself and your children to a 45-minute cruise on Monterey Bay. You will most likely encounter sea lions, fishing boats, and beautiful views (adults $5, 6–11 $4, under 6 free). Or you may want to try your hand at deep sea fishing. Children are welcome, and Sam

encourages beginners to join him on weekends and holidays at 7:30am (adults $17, under 12 $7, fishing pole $3.50, bait furnished).

SIGHTSEEING CRUISES:

Monterey Fishing Trips, *408/373-3501; daily in summer, weekends rest of year; adults $2.50, 6–11 $1.50, under 6 free; reservations not necessary.*

Frank's Fishing Trips, *408/372-2203, same hours and rates as above.* Both offer 30-minute cruises around Monterey Bay.

Jacks Peak Stables, *550 Aguajito Rd., 408/375-4232; $10/hour; Tu–Sun from 9:30am, closed M.* Over 50 miles of beautiful forest trails await you and your hired horse. Riding lessons can be arranged. Call ahead for reservations and details.

Les Josselyn Bicycles, *638 Lighthouse, 408/649-8520; $6–$8/day.* Rent 3-speed and 10-speed bicycles here and head out to Cannery Row and Pacific Grove.

Monterey State Historic Park, *115 Alvarado St., 408/373-2103; daily 9am–5pm; 50¢.* Part of the California State Park System, this park consists of ten historical sites and preserved adobes. The fee admits you to all of the buildings. Begin your tour and gather information at the Custom House located at 1 Custom House Plaza.

California's First Theater, *Scott/Pacific, 408/375-4916; 8pm curtain W, Th, Sun, 8:30pm curtain F & Sat; adults $4, 13–18 $3, under 13 $2.* Children over age five will enjoy visiting this ex-saloon and boarding house for sailors. The first play was presented in 1847, and the "Troupers of the Gold Coast" are still going strong. Nowadays the melodramatic shows and olios change periodically, but they are still presented in the tiny theater just like they were in the old days— only now the snacks served at the old oak bar in the lobby are soda pop. Best seating for kids is on the benches in the back, though the little tables in front are tempting. Call for reservations and current schedule.

U.S. Army Museum, *at the Presidio, 408/242-8547; Th–M 9am–12:30, 1:30–4pm, closed Tu & W; free.* The history of "Old Fort" Hill is told through dioramas, artifacts, and photographs. Next to the museum are ten historic sites including a 2,000-year-old Indian village site and ceremonial "rain rock," the ruins of Fort Mervine, and the site of Father Serra's 1770 landing.

Scuba Diving. This area is legend with scuba divers. If you would like to take a few lessons or rent some equipment while you're visiting, contact:
Aquarius Dive School, *2240 Del Monte Blvd., 408/375-1933.*
Monterey Dive Center, *763 Lighthouse Ave., 408/375-6363.*
Monterey Peninsula Dive Club, *871 Foam St., 408/373-1377.*

PACIFIC GROVE

Pacific Grove Chamber of Commerce
P.O. Box 167
(Forest/Central Aves.)
Pacific Grove 93950
408/373-3304

■ *SPECIAL EVENTS*
Every year in late October hundreds of thousands of Monarch butterflies return to Pacific Grove to winter on the needles of favored local pine trees. There they dangle in huge clusters and are often mistaken for pieces of bark. They migrate all the way from western Canada and Alaska and stay until March when they again fly north.

Somewhat of a mystery is how they find their way here each year since, with a lifespan of less than a year, no butterfly makes the trip twice. The stunning orange and black Monarchs somehow pass this information on to their progeny which then return to these same trees the following fall and repeat the cycle.

Monarchs like to flutter about on sunny days between the hours of 10am and 4pm, which is the best time to view them. On cold and foggy days, which are quite common in this area, they cling to the trees and keep their wings closed—reacting to the weather somewhat like a golden poppy. Be sure not to bother these fragile, lovely creatures . . . in Pacific Grove it is a crime, carrying a $500 fine, to molest a butterfly.

To celebrate the annual return of the butterflies, the town of Pacific Grove (Butterfly Town, USA) hosts a special parade each year. School children dress up as butterflies and march along with the more traditional bands and majorette corps. Afterwards the local PTA sponsors a bazaar and carnival where celebrants can enjoy old-fashioned fun and homemade food. For the current year's date, contact the Chamber of Commerce.

In March there is a Victorian Home Tour. Children under 12 are not permitted. Take your teenagers. Check with the Chamber of Commerce for the current year's date.

- *CHILDCARE*
  Asilomar maintains a list of local sitters. Call 408/372-8016.

- *WHERE TO STAY*

  Asilomar, *800 Asilomar Blvd. (P.O. Box 537), 408/372-8016; $15–$30;
  cribs, pool, game lounge; some TVs, kitchens, ocean views, and fireplaces.* Though this facility is used mainly as a conference grounds,

it is part of the California State Park System and, when they are underbooked, rentals are made to the general public. Reservations may not be made more than one week in advance; often there are last minute accommodations available. The name Asilomar means literally "refuge by the sea." It is located in a quiet, scenic area just a short walk from the ocean. For a reasonable charge, guests may join in conference meals at 7:30am, noon, and 6pm.

Beachcomber Inn, *1996 Sunset, 408/373-4769, toll-free reservations 800/453-4511; $25.50–$35.50; cribs, pool, free bikes, color TV, sauna, free use of beach blankets; some waterbeds, ocean views, and kitchens.* This oceanfront motel is a bit off the beaten track and makes for a pleasant retreat.

Bide-a-Wee Motel, *221 Asilomar Blvd., 408/372-2330; $18.* Owned by *Rip* and Judy *Van Winkle*!!, every room in this sleepy motel is different.

Butterfly Trees Lodge, *1150 Lighthouse Ave., 408/372-0503; $32–$34; some kitchens.* Located adjacent to a favorite butterfly nesting spot, this is an attractive and quiet motel.

Milar Butterfly Grove Motel, *1073 Lighthouse Ave., 408/373-4921; $20–$35; pool, TV, cribs; some waterbeds and kitchens.* Two acres of landscaped grounds and close proximity to some of the butterfly's favorite trees make this a choice spot to stay. There is a school playground located directly across the quiet side street this motel is located on.

Pebble Beach Rentals, *1130 Wildcat Canyon Rd., Pebble Beach 93953; 408/625-1400; $100/weekend.* Stay in a modern condominium in the beautiful Pebble Beach forest.

17 Mile Drive Village, *17 Mile Drive/Sinex Ave., 408/373-2721; $15–$18; pool, jacuzzi, some RV hookups, dining facilities, two-night minimum on weekends, some TVs.* Though in no way luxurious, this is an inexpensive place to sleep and good to know about if you are having trouble finding more aesthetic lodging. Eighty vintage cottages are scattered in a clearing of huge pine trees. The pool and jacuzzi allow for a refreshing dip in a lovely outdoor setting.

Motel Row. Numerous motels are located at the west end of Lighthouse Ave. and on Asilomar Blvd.

■ WHERE TO EAT

Golden West Pancakes, *701 Lighthouse, 408/375-5101; open daily 24 hours; highchairs, booster seats, children's portions.* Offering a typical pancake house atmosphere and menu, this is a good stop for breakfast and is very popular with local residents. The special children's menu allows kids to pick their meal from inviting photographs.

■ *WHAT TO DO*

Bicycle Rentals, *Beachcomber Inn, $1.50 for up to three hours.*

Bicycle Trips, *Velco Club Monterey, 408/372-2552.* A trip departs at 10am every Sunday from the Monterey Youth Center. Call for details.

See the Butterflies. The densest clusters of Monarchs occur at **Milar's Butterfly Grove Motel.** Other good viewing spots are the **Butterfly Trees Lodge** and **George Washington Park** at Short/Adler Sts. A statue honoring the butterfly is located at **Lover's Point**; a few butterflies can occasionally be seen fluttering there.

Golf. Call 408/624-3811 for current information on availability of tee times and course conditions.

Lover's Point Marina, *626 Ocean View Blvd., 408/373-3304.* Glass bottom boats, first introduced here in 1892 and now operated by the Chamber of Commerce, take 30-minute trips during the summer (adults $2.25, under 14 $1.75). The trip gives you a chance to see the marine life which attracts scientists from all over the world. Row boats, motor boats, pedal boats, and other water paraphernalia are available for rent. There is also a pleasant beach for sunbathing and wading as well as a grassy picnic area with barbecue pits.

Pacific Grove Museum of Natural History, *165 Forest Ave., 408/372-4212; Tu-Sun 10am-5pm, closed M; free.* The natural history of Monterey County is displayed here. See exhibits of butterflies, marine and bird life, native plants, shells, and Indian artifacts.

Point Piños Lighthouse, *on Asilomar Blvd., about two blocks north of the end of Lighthouse Ave., 408/373-3304; weekends and holidays 2-4pm; free.* The Coast Guard gives guided tours of this oldest of Pacific Coast lighthouses, built in 1855. This is a good spot for walking, picnicking, and observing sea otters.

Pebble Beach Equestrian Center, *Portola Rd., Pebble Beach, 408/624-2756; $10/hour; group rides daily 10am & 2pm; reservations required.* It's strictly English saddles here. Lessons are available. The extensive bridle trails wind through lovely Del Monte Forest.

Seventeen Mile Drive, *408/372-5813; $4/car.* There are three entrances to this famous drive: Pacific Grove (off Sunset), Carmel Hill (off Hwy 1), and Carmel (Scenic Dr.). The scenery is a combination of showplace homes, world-famous golf courses, raw seascapes, and wildlife. Short walks can be enjoyed in several spots, the most famous being Cypress Walk. If you're here at dusk, you'll see great numbers of deer out for their evening feeding. If you want to splurge and have lunch or dinner at the elegant **Lodge At Pebble Beach,** your $4 gate fee will be deducted from the bill. By the way, the drive no longer measures 17 miles; it is now shorter.

"Poor Man's" Seventeen Mile Drive. There is no charge for this scenic drive. Take Ocean View Blvd. to Point Piños and then turn left on Sunset Dr. You will see rugged seascapes and old Victorian homes. From April to August the beautiful lavender ice plant (mesembryanthemum) cascades in full bloom over the rocky beach front.

CARMEL

Carmel Business Association
P.O. Box 4444
(Vandervort Court on San Carlos/Ocean)
Carmel 93921
408/624-2522

■ *SPECIAL EVENTS*
Bach Festival, *July. Write: P.O. Box 575, Carmel 93921, 408/624-1521.*

■ *A LITTLE BACKGROUND*
A well-established weekend retreat, Carmel is best known for its abundant shops, cozy lodging, and picturesque beach. It is also known for the things which it doesn't have: few sidewalks or street signs and no streetlights, house numbers, neon signs, jukeboxes, or buildings over two stories high. These absent items help Carmel to keep its small-town feeling.

Because Carmel is a popular weekend destination, it is important to make reservations for your accommodations far in advance—especially if you want to stay in one of its interesting inns. It seems that almost every weekend some special tournament, race, or house tour is scheduled—making available lodging scarce.

■ *WHERE TO STAY*
Carmel River Inn, *26600 Oliver Rd., 93923, 408/624-1575; $28–$32; cribs, color TV, pool; some fireplaces and kitchens.* Located on ten acres and offering a choice of motel rooms or individual cottages, this inn has plenty of grassy space for children to romp and explore.

The Green Lantern, *7th/Casanova Sts. (P.O. Box 1114), 408/624-4392; $24–$50; cribs, some kitchens, fireplaces, and cottages.* Located on a quiet side street, this is a pleasant rustic spot to stay.

Highlands Inn, *P.O. Box 1700, toll-free reservations 800/682-4811; $96–$130; cribs, includes breakfast and dinner.* Located on the scenic outskirts of town, this legendary inn appears at first to be outrageously expensive. When you consider that two of your meals are included in the price and that the accommodations are truly luxurious, the price begins to seem a little more reasonable—at least for a splurge. The spectacular setting and choice of lanai rooms or cottages make the Highlands Inn a place you'll want to visit. And remember—the Beatles slept here.

December is a special month here and is celebrated with a Scottish Christmas tree ceremony on December 7, the laying of the yule log on Christmas eve, and a traditional Christmas dinner on Christmas day. On New Year's Eve there is a wassail bowl and Hogmanay Ball and dinner and a special dinner on New Year's Day.

Holiday House, *Camino Real/7th (P.O. Box 234), 408/624-6267; $18–$26; cribs, breakfast and afternoon tea included.* Styled in the fashion of a European pension, this large old Carmel home built in 1906 has been a guest house for over 30 years. A few rooms open into the garden and are especially suited to families. Babysitting can be arranged. It is very quiet here and only a short walk to the beach.

The Homestead, *Lincoln/8th Ave. (P.O. Box 1285), 408/624-4119; $25–$28; color TV.* Resembling a red farmhouse more than a Carmel hideaway, The Homestead has a comfortable, informal feeling that makes it attractive to families.

Lamp Lighters Inn, *Ocean Ave./Camino Real (P.O. Box 604), 408/624-7372; $35–$145.* This gingerbread village features charming cottages and rooms and a convenient location between the shops and the ocean. It will surely fill your fairytale fantasies and maybe even your children's.

Normandy Inn, *Ocean Ave./Monte Verde (P.O. Box 1706), 408/624-3825; $47; cribs, pool, breakfast included, some color TVs.* Continental breakfasts are served to guests in the French Provincial kitchen located off the lobby. Accommodations are luxurious and include a choice of Normandy-style hotel rooms, suites, and cottages.

Ocean View Lodge, *P.O. Box 3696, 408/624-7723; $50; cribs, color TV, kitchens, ocean views, fireplaces, some private porches.* Rooms are decorated in Early American style.

Pine Inn, *Ocean/Monte Verde (P.O. Box 250), 408/624-3851; $40–$75; cribs, dining facilities, some views.* Claiming to be the oldest hotel in Carmel, the Pine Inn is elegantly decorated in the Victorian mode and features many rooms with ocean views. Room service is available for breakfast.

■ *WHERE TO EAT*

The Butcher Shop, *Ocean/Dolores, 408/624-2569; Sun-Th 4:30–10pm,
F & Sat 4:30–11pm; booster seats, children's portions.* This serious
dining room serves corn-fed Kansas beef as well as Australian lobster
tail and other seafood delicacies. Dinners include a relish bowl,
shrimp salad, and hot cheese/bacon bread. Children's dinners are a
choice of prime rib, chopped sirloin, or fish.

Carmel Kitchen, *Ocean Ave./Carmel Plaza, 408/624-4433; daily 7am–
8pm; highchairs, booster seats.* Here it is, an ordinary coffee shop in
the middle of expensive Carmel. Royal Kona coffee and breakfast
are served all day.

Cottage of Sweets, *Ocean Ave./Lincoln (P.O. Box 5935), 408/624-5170.*
Among the sweet surprises in this gingerbread cottage are imported
candies and chocolates, diet candy, gourmet jelly beans, and taffy.

Em Le's, *Dolores/5th, 408/624-2905; open daily; highchairs, booster
seats.* Cozy and crowded, Em Le's serves a huge variety of breakfast
items at very reasonable prices. With its lace curtains and views of
the sidewalk, this diner comes across with a very special Carmel fla-
vor. The buttermilk waffles and blueberry pancakes are my personal
favorites.

The Harbinger, *Ocean/Mission in Carmel Plaza, 408/625-1483; daily
11am–4pm, 5:30–10pm; booster seats.* When the sun is shining, head
for the sylvan patio of the Harbinger for lunch. Choose from hamburgers and sandwiches for lunch and continental specialties such as
roast duckling flambé, scampi, and filet mignon for dinner. Inside
dining is also available.

Hector De Smet Bakery, *Ocean Ave./Lincoln; daily 6:30am–8pm.* Caramel apples, cookie monster cupcakes, and alligators and turtles made
of marzipan bread are just a few of the delicacies available at this
popular bakery. A large selection of pastries and drinks are also available, and all may be enjoyed on the premises or as you walk the
boutique-laden Carmel streets.

Hog's Breath Inn, *San Carlos/5th, 408/625-1044; Sunday brunch 11am–
2pm, daily 11:30am–3pm, 6–11pm; booster seats, children's portions.*
Owned by actor Clint Eastwood, this rustic secluded spot features a
casual, cozy atmosphere. Many tables are located outdoors under a
rambling old oak tree and are warmed by fireplaces when the tem-
perature chills. Sunday brunch is especially good for families; the
menu offers such items as Thunderbolt (cheese omelette), Clint's
Special (artichoke omelette), and Magnum Force (hamburger omelette). If your kids aren't reliably well-behaved, avoid bringing them
here.

Mediterranean Market, *Ocean/Mission; daily 9am–6pm.* At this well-stocked delicatessen you can choose from such treats as freshly marinated artichoke hearts, exotic beers, and skinny French baguettes as well as such standards as sandwich meats, cheeses, soft drinks, and wines. You can even purchase gourmet items such as caviar—and a picnic basket to carry it all away in. Located practically next door is **Wisharts Bakery** (M–Sat 9am–6pm, closed Sun) where all kinds of tasty desserts and fresh breads are available. After you've selected your luncheon supplies, head out to the beach for a peaceful picnic.

Mrs. M's Fudge, *Mission/6th (P.O. Box 3213), 408/624-5331; daily until 9pm.* Seventeen flavors of homemade fudge and unusual "snow fruit" (apricots, peaches, pears, cherries, and walnut-stuffed prunes dipped in white chocolate) are just a few of the diet-deserting goodies available here.

Rocky Point Restaurant, *12 miles south of Carmel on Hwy 1 (P.O. Box 6446), 408/624-2933; Tu–Sun 5:30–10pm, closed M; highchairs, booster seats, children's portions; reservations essential.* Take a scenic drive down the coast toward Big Sur, and stop at the Rocky Point for a steak or seafood dinner. The spectacular view is included in the steep menu prices.

Swedish Restaurant, *Dolores/7th, 408/624-3723; daily 8am–8:30pm, in winter closed on Tu; booster seats.* This tiny cheerful spot is my favorite stop for breakfast. A large window allows diners to view the busy sidewalk, and a fireplace warms the room. Portions are generous and reasonably priced. The Swedish lingonberry pancakes are excellent.

Thunderbird, *Hwy 1/Rio Rd. in the Barnyard, 408/624-1803; daily 11am–3:30pm, Tu & F 5:30–8pm, Sat to 9pm; highchairs, booster seats, children's portions.* Dine among world-famous authors in this combination bookstore/restaurant. Dinners change every evening and are served with soup or salad and popovers.

■ WHAT TO DO

The Basilica of Mission San Carlos Borromeo del Rio Carmelo, *Rio Rd. west of Hwy 1, 408/624-3600; M–Sat 9:30am–5pm, Sun & holidays 10:30am–5pm, services on Sunday; free, donations welcome.* The mission was established by Father Junipero Serra in 1770. He is buried here at the foot of the altar. The mission houses a museum store where you can see Indian artifacts, mission tools, the original mission kitchen, and California's first library. A charming courtyard garden accents the cemetery where over 3,000 mission Indians were buried. A fiesta is held each year on the last Sunday in September.

BEACHES:

    Carmel Beach, *at the foot of Ocean Ave.* This world-famous beach, known for its white powdery sand and spectacular sunsets, is a choice spot for a refreshing walk, a picnic, or flying a kite. A sand castle contest is held here annually in October (contact the Carmel Business Association for details). */Swimming is unsafe.*

    Carmel River State Beach, *at the end of Scenic Rd.* Very popular with families, this fresh-water lagoon is also a bird sanctuary. There are picnic facilities and open fires are allowed.

    San Jose Creek. Scuba divers come from all over to enjoy the underworld beauty of Carmel Bay. This is one of their favorite diving spots and a good place to watch them while you enjoy a picnic.

Brass Rubbing Centre, *Mission/8th (P.O. Box 4926); 408/624-2990; M–Sat 10:30am–5pm, Sun by appointment.* It used to be that people would travel to England to make wax-on-paper impressions of the brass plaques embedded in the floors of old churches. Recently the brasses have become so worn that this practice is now forbidden. But now this inexpensive hobby can be enjoyed in shops like this one, where you can make rubbings of reproductions.

Come Fly a Kite, *in Carmel Plaza.* If the kids forgot their kites, you can pick one up here and then head for the beach—the perfect spot to launch it.

Dansk II, *Ocean Ave., open daily.* You can get up to 66 percent off on discontinued Dansk items and seconds. I'm throwing this in for all of you who like to cook and appreciate this expensive line of merchandise.

Forest Theater in the Ground, *Mountain View/Santa Rita, 408/624-1531; F, Sat, Sun 8:30pm; adults $4.50, children $2.50; reservations suggested.* Dance, music, and drama performances are held in this unique outdoor theater. Call for the current schedule.

Point Lobos State Reserve, *located off Hwy 1 a few miles south of Car-*

mel (Route 1 Box 62), Carmel 93923, 408/624-4909; $2/car. Here
you have the opportunity to see the rustic, undeveloped beauty of the
Monterey Peninsula. Described as "the greatest meeting of land and
water in the world," Point Lobos offers self-guiding trails as well as
guided ranger walks. Sea otters may often be seen in the reserve's

waters. Be sure to dress warmly, and bring along your binoculars and camera and maybe a picnic too.

Take a Ride to Carmel Valley. Follow Carmel Valley Rd. to the Carmel Valley Village. Backtrack and take Laureles Grade north and then Hwy 68 west to Monterey. On this scenic drive you will pass begonia gardens, regional parks, the Laguna Seca Raceway, and the tasting room of the Monterey Peninsula Winery.

Thinker Toys, *Carmel Plaza (P.O. Box 6297), 408/624-0441; M–Sat 9:30am–9pm, Sun 10am–5:30pm.* This is a super toy store. It offers an exciting selection of puppets, dolls, workbooks, and puzzles. An annex in another part of the plaza houses a large selection of model trains. Bring your kids here to purchase a souvenir.

SIDE TRIP:

SALINAS

Salinas Visitor and Convention Bureau
P.O. Box 1170
(119 E. Alisal)
Salinas 93902
408/424-7611

For 50¢ you can order a ten-page booklet which describes the points of interest in downtown Salinas and outlines four one-day self-guided tours.

■ *GETTING THERE*

Note that you can also get to Salinas on Amtrak from Oakland (8:50am) and San Jose (10:06am) and return the same day.

■ *WHERE TO EAT*

The Steinbeck House, *132 Central Ave., 93901, 408/424-2735; M–F seatings at 11:45am & 1:15pm; highchairs, booster seats; reservations suggested.* In 1902 John Steinbeck was born in the front bedroom of this Victorian house. Now the house is run by the Valley Guild, a volunteer organization, as a gourmet luncheon restaurant specializing in serving seasonal produce grown in the Salinas Valley. The menu changes each day and includes such items as ratatouille crepes, poulet de asparagus, and chicken-artichoke crepes. After lunch you can browse through antiques and Steinbeck's books in the gift shop located downstairs and/or take a short walk down a street lined with lovely old Victorian homes to the nearby Steinbeck Library.

■ *WHAT TO DO*

Peter Paul Candy Factory, *1800 S. Abbott, 408/424-0481; 30-minute tours on Tu & Th at 10am, other times by appointment; free.* If your children are age 8 or older, you should treat them to a tour of this candy factory. After seeing all the huge containers of tasty ingredients and watching the candy-producing process, visitors are treated to free samples.

BIG SUR

■ *ROUTE*

Located approximately 155 miles south of San Francisco. Take Hwy 101 to Hwy 17 to Hwy 1.

■ *WHERE TO STAY*

Big Sur Lodge, *408/667-2171; $32–$44; pool, sauna, recreation room, dining facilities; some fireplaces and kitchens.* Located in Pfeiffer-Big Sur State Park, this facility offers lodging in cabins and rooms and use of the park's ranger-led nature walks, campfires, river swimming, and nature exhibits.

Glen Oaks Motel, *408/667-2105; $28–$30.* This is a modern motel.

Ripplewood Resort, *408/667-2242; $20–$50; some kitchens.* Rustic redwood cabins are located both above and below the highway. The ones below are more expensive but are also only a stone's throw from the river.

■ *WHERE TO CAMP*

Ventana Campground, *408/667-2331; $6/night.* Lovely, secluded sites are available in this private campground. A store and deli are nearby.

■ *WHERE TO EAT*

Big Sur Inn, *408/667-2377; highchairs, booster seats.* Though lunch and dinner are served, my favorite meal here is breakfast—especially when it's raining outside and I manage to secure a table in front of the fireplace. The mellow, rustic setting is a perfect background for the fresh, simple foods which are produced by the kitchen. Rustic lodging is also available.

Nepenthe, *408/667-2345; daily; highchairs; reservations suggested.* On the fancy side, this restaurant is located at the top of a crest and offers a breathtaking view of the coast. It is said that John F. Kennedy was turned away from here when he was a senator because he wasn't wearing shoes. Take heed.

■ *WHAT TO DO*

Big Sur is so non-commercial that there is nothing to list in this section. Note, also, that there is no TV in Big Sur. Bring along a good book and relax, swim in the river, picnic on the beach, or take a hike through the woods.

SAN SIMEON — HEARST CASTLE

San Simeon Chamber of Commerce Visitors Bureau
P.O. Box 1
(Hwy 1)
San Simeon 93452
(805/927-3500

■ *GETTING THERE*

For a leisurely trip to Hearst Castle, try the train package offered by **Great Western Tours** (Sheraton-Palace Hotel, San Francisco 94105, 415/398-2996). Remember, this is the way guests used to travel to the castle; invitations always included train tickets. For $85/person you can relax and enjoy the scenery while Amtrak's Coast Starlight transports you to San Luis Obispo. There you will be transferred to a bus for a lectured sightseeing tour to the coast and the San Simeon Lodge, where you will spend the night. The next day you will be bussed to the famed castle for a guided tour, then down scenic Hwy 1 to the fishing village of Morro Bay, and then back to San Luis Obispo for the trip home. The package price does not include meals.

A similar tour, via bus instead of train, is offered by **California Parlor Car Tours** (Jack Tar Hotel, Van Ness/Geary, San Francisco 94101, 415/495-1444). The price is $183 per adult and $163 per child for two nights and three days. Meals are included. Call for further details.

■ *A LITTLE BACKGROUND*

Located in the small town of San Simeon on the wind-blown coast south of Big Sur, the spectacular Hearst Castle is perched atop La Cuesta Encantada (the enchanted hill) and is filled with art treasures and antiques from all over the world. Though considered by Hearst to be unfinished, the castle contains 38 bedrooms, 31 bathrooms, 14 sitting rooms, a kitchen, a movie theater, 2 libraries, a billiard room, a dining hall, and an assembly hall! Exotic vines and plants inhabit the lovely gardens, and wild animals such as zebras, goats, and sheep still graze the hillsides—remnants of his private zoo which included lions, monkeys, and a polar bear.

Before 1958 visitors could get no closer than was permitted by the coin-operated telescope located on the road below. Operated now by the State of California as a Historical Monument, the castle is now open to the public. Three tours are available; all include a scenic bus ride up to the castle.

Reservations for the castle tours are essential and may be made at most Ticketron terminals. Be prepared to pay cash. In the San Francisco area call 415/393-6914 for information.

Reservations may also be made by mail. For an order form write: Ticketron, P.O. Box 26430, San Francisco 94126. Tickets may be ordered up to eight weeks in advance. The charge for each tour is: adults $5, 6–17 $2.50. Send the fee plus 80¢ service charge per ticket. Tickets may also be purchased at the castle after 8am on the day of the tour. However, often none are available. When they are available, they are usually sold out before noon.

Tour 1, Enchanted Hill Tour, is suggested for the first visit and includes gardens, pools, a guest house, and the main floor of the castle.

Tour 2, La Casa Grande Tour, is a guided tour through 26 rooms on the upper floors of the castle, including Mr. Hearst's private suite, the libraries, and the kitchen.

Tour 3, New Wing Tour, is a guided tour through the North Wing and includes gardens, pools, and a guest house.

Note: Children under 6 are free only if they sit on their parents' lap on the bus ride. You will be walking about ½ mile and climbing approximately 300 steps on each tour; wear comfortable shoes. Tours take approximately two hours. Strollers, food, flash equipment, and smoking are not allowed.

■ *ROUTE*

Located approximately 220 miles south of San Francisco. Take Hwy 101 to Hwy 17 to Hwy 1.

■ *WHERE TO STAY*

Cambria Shores Motel, *P.O. Box 63, San Simeon 93452, 805/927-4107; $29–$37; color TV, ocean views, direct access to beach; open in summer only.*

Green Tree Inn Motel, *P.O. Box 68, San Simeon 93452, 805/927-4691; toll-free reservations 800/528-1234; $38; TV, indoor pool, family room, continental breakfast included, dining facilities; open in summer only.*

San Simeon Pines Resort Motel, *P.O. Box 115, San Simeon 93452, 805/927-4648; $28–$40; TV, pool, playground, golf course, special family section, private access to beach.*

Sea Shore Motel, *6180 Moonstone Beach Dr., Cambria 93428, 805/927-4422; $25–$35; cribs, TV, play area for children, some ocean views; open in summer only.*

Silver Surf Motel, *Route 1, Box 210, San Simeon 93452, 805/927-4662; toll-free reservations 800/453-4511; $30–$38; cribs, family rooms, indoor pool, ocean views, playground, putting green, dining facilities, some color TVs.*

■ *WHERE TO EAT*

Brambles Dinner House, *4005 Burton Dr., Cambria 93428, 805/927-4716; daily 5–10pm; children's portions; reservations suggested.* Fish, steaks, and lobster dominate the menu. The restaurant is located inside an English cottage.

Cottage of Sweets, *Plaza del Cavalier, San Simeon, 805/927-3262.* Enjoy

an ice cream soda at the fountain or purchase imported candies for a sweet snack.

Grey Fox Inn, *4095 Burton Dr., Cambria 93428, 805/927-3305; daily 11:30am–3pm, 5:30–9:30pm, Sunday brunch 9am–2pm, closed M & Tu in winter; children's portions; reservations suggested.* This converted home offers delightful meals and terrace dining. Entrees change daily.

Sebastian's General Store, *P.O. Box 133, San Simeon 93452, 805/927-*

4217; store: daily *8:30am–6pm, cafe: daily 8:30am–8pm.* Built in 1852 and moved to its present location in 1878, Sebastian's is now a state historical landmark. The cafe serves inexpensive short orders for breakfast and lunch, and there is a pleasant outdoor patio where you may eat.

■ WHAT TO DO

Bleschyu Miniature Golf Park, *Hwy 1, San Simeon, 805/927-4165.* A game arcade rounds out the offerings at this facility.

Coast Pedalers, *Cambria.* Tandem bikes may be rented as well as 3-speeds and 10-speeds.

Nitwit Ridge, *located in the western section of Cambria Pines.* "Organic" architecture may be seen in this home which was put together a piece at a time (using stones, seashells, odds and ends) over a period of 40 years.

The Soldier Factory, *789 Main St., Cambria 93428, 805/927-3804; open daily.* The majority of items sold in this shop are designed, molded, and cast on the premises. Paper castles and forts as well as chess sets and assorted sizes and styles of tin soldiers are for sale. A very interesting museum is housed in the back. This is an ideal souvenir stop.

MORRO BAY

Morro Bay Chamber of Commerce
213 Beach St.
Morro Bay 93442
805/772-4467

■ SPECIAL EVENTS

Fire Muster, *September.* Teams of firemen compete in everything from bucket brigades to hose-cart races to hook-and-ladder climbing. There is even a parade of antique fire-fighting equipment and an old-fashioned Fireman's Ball. Contact the Chamber of Commerce for details or 805/772-2737.

■ A LITTLE BACKGROUND

The huge volcanic rock, visible from just about everywhere in town, is the reason Morro Bay is sometimes called "the Gibraltar of the Pacific." It stands 576 feet high and is now a state monument. Commercial fishing is the number one industry here, with albacore and abalone the specialties.

- *ROUTE*
  Located approximately 235 miles south of San Francisco.
  Take Hwy 101 to Hwy 17 to Hwy 1.

- *WHERE TO STAY IN TOWN*
  Breakers Motel, *Morro Bay Blvd./Market Ave. (P.O. Box 110), 805/772-7317; $30–$46; color TV, pool; some ocean views and fireplaces.*
  Harbor View Motor Lodge, *215 Harbor St., 805/772-2447; $16–$25; ocean views, color TV, enclosed pool, cribs, some kitchens.*
  Log Cabin Motel, *851 Market Ave., 805/772-7132; $15–$28; cribs, color TV; some ocean views and cabins.*
  Point Motel, *3450 Toro Lane, 805/772-2053; $14–$26; TV, kitchens, views, beach access.*
  San Marcos Motel, *250 Pacific St., 805/772-2248, toll-free reservations 800/528-1234; $34; cribs, color TV, fireplaces, some ocean views.*
  Sundown Motel, *640 Main, 805/772-7381; $18–$24; cribs, TV.*

- *WHERE TO STAY NEARBY*
  Sunnybrook Farm and Country Inn, *P.O. Box 95, Paso Robles 93446, 805/238-5534; rates vary according to age and time of year, adults $40–$46/person; two night minimum, playground, recreation barn, pool, tennis courts, sauna, hot tub.* Visitors stay in comfortable modern cottages while visiting this farm. Family-style meals made from produce grown right on the farm, hayrides, campfires, hikes,

bicycles, swimming, fishing, and helping with the farm chores are in-cluded in the rates. For an additional fee you can rent horses and boats and enroll children in an activity program.

■ WHERE TO EAT

Breakers Cafe, *801 Market St., 805/772-7323; open for breakfast and lunch; highchairs, booster seats.* This casual restaurant features good views and hearty breakfasts (omelettes, pancakes, waffles).

Galley Restaurant, *899 Embarcadero, 805/772-2806; daily 11:30am–9pm, closed in December; highchairs, booster seats, children's por-tions; reservations essential.* This extremely popular restaurant offers great ocean views. Seafood dinners dominate the menu, but chicken, pork chops, steak, salads, sandwiches, and hamburgers are also available.

Grimsby Trading Co. Deli, *650 Morro Bay Blvd., 805/772-3000.* Pick up your picnic supplies here.

Rose's Landing, *725 Embarcadero, 805/772-4441; M-F 4–10pm, Sat & Sun 11:30am–10pm; children's portions; reservations essential.* Good views and food make this restaurant extremely popular. Seafood and steaks dominate the menu, but you can also get a hamburger. I sug-gest taking only well-behaved children.

The Whale's Tail, *945 Embarcadero, 805/772-7555.* The inexpensive menu features soups, salads, assorted seafood 'n chips, hamburgers, and sandwiches. A cioppino (shellfish stew) is available on Thurs-day evenings.

Zeke's Wharf, *701 Embarcadero, 805/772-2269; open for lunch and din-ner; highchairs, booster seats.* Zeke's is inexpensive and casual and offers great views of the water and "rock." Lunch and dinner fea-tures seafood items as well as sandwiches, "dogs on a stick," and hamburgers.

■ WHAT TO DO IN TOWN

Bird Sanctuary, *south of Morro Bay State Park.* Following a trail through the marsh and hills allows you to catch possible glimpses of over 250 species of birds. This is the third largest bird sanctuary in the world.

Centennial Stairway/Giant Chess, *located in the center of the Embarca-dero, 805/772-7329.* At the stairway's base is one of the largest chess-boards ever constructed. The redwood pawns stand two feet tall. Pieces weigh from 18 to 30 pounds, making a game here physical as well as mental exercise. At noon each Saturday the Morro Bay Chess Club sponsors chess on the giant 16 x 16 foot concrete board. The board is available to the public daily from 8am to 5 pm. Reservations for use must be made before noon at least one day in advance. Weekend reservations must be made by noon Friday. Reservations for using the adjoining shuffleboard are made similarly.

Clamdigging. Go to it! World-famous Pismo clams may be dug up just about anywhere.

Fishing. Fish from the pier, or go out on a chartered fishing boat.

Heron Rookery. This is one of the last rookeries where the Great Blue Heron may be found. No one is allowed inside the rookery, but the herons may be viewed from a special observation area which has informative displays.

Morro Bay Aquarium, *595 Embarcadero, 805/772-7647; daily 10am–5pm; adults 70¢, 6–12 35¢, under 6 free.* Over 300 live marine specimens are available for observation, and you can feed the seals. There are also some preserved specimens.

Morro Rock Playground, *east of Morro Rock.* Children will enjoy this playground in the sand.

Museum of Natural History, *White Point in Morro Bay State Park; daily 10am–5pm; adults 50¢, 6–17 25¢, under 6 free.* This museum features displays, lectures, slide shows, and movies on the wildlife and Indian history of the area. Guided tours are given on weekends.

Tiger's Folly Harbor Cruises, *on the Embarcadero, 805/772-2255; adults $2.50, children $1.* One-hour cruises leave at noon, 2, 4, and 6pm daily in the summer, weekends in the winter.

■ *WHAT TO DO NEARBY*

Avila Beach, *20 miles south of town off Hwy 101.* This tiny, old-fashioned beach community is a great place to watch surfers and swim in a generally mild surf. There is a playground, a pier, and many tiny diners. Notable is the **Seaside Cafe** where you can enjoy homemade fish and shrimp tacos, tangy chile verde burritos, and great guacamole. On the way to or from the beach, you may want to stop at either the **Sycamore Mineral Springs** (805/595-7302) where you can rent a hot tub or **Avila Hot Springs** (805/595-2359) where you can rent inner tubes to use in the warm pool.

Cayucos, *six miles north of town on Hwy 1.* Cayucos has a fine beach, the surf is gentle, and there is a great children's playground. Fishing may be enjoyed from the pier and rocks; equipment may be rented at **Al's Sporting Goods** on N. Ocean Ave. Try lunch at **The Way Station,** a nineteenth century traveler's rest stop once again functioning as such, at 74 N. Ocean Ave.

Diablo Canyon Nuclear Information Center, *P.O. Box 592, San Luis Obispo 93401, 805/595-2327; free.* See the Ecology Room with fish and wildlife exhibits, the Nuclear Theater where you can watch the story of man's progress from the discovery of fire to nuclear power (three screens and stereo sound), the Future Clock where you can see a slide show of the world as it might be ten years from now, and the Archaeology Exhibit showing utensils and weapons of former inhabitants of the area. A free 1½ hour bus tour to the overlook of the Diablo Canyon Nuclear Power Plant may be taken if you make advance reservations.

Gum Alley, *next to 733 Higuera, San Luis Obispo.* This vulgar, tacky eyesore is a cheap thrill for gum-loving children. For over ten years people have been depositing their gum on these brick walls. Some have even taken the time to make designs. It reminded me of what the bottom of a school desk might look like. Gumless? Drop in to **Cook's Variety,** an old-fashioned dime store located at 725 Higuera. There you can choose from a wide selection of gums (the 2¢ "Double Bubble" is said to stick the best), chew a bit, and then leave your mark.

Mission San Luis Obispo de Tolosa, *Chorro/Monterey Sts., San Luis Obispo; Tu–Sun 9am–5pm, closed M; admission 50¢, $1/family.* Built in 1772, this is referred to as "the Prince of Missions." There is also a museum and gardens. Nearby is the Murray Historical Adobe, the County Historical Museum (W–Sun 10am–noon, 1–4pm; free) and the Art Center (daily noon–5pm).

Montana de Oro State Park, *5 miles south of Morro Bay.* You may indulge in primitive camping, picnic, swim, or hike on over 5,600 acres of undeveloped land.

SOLVANG

Solvang Business Association
P.O. Box 465
(1623 Mission Dr.)
Solvang 93463
805/688-3317

■ *SPECIAL EVENTS*

Theatrefest. Summer theater begins the last weekend in June. Contact Pacific Conservatory of the Performing Arts, P.O. Box 1389, Santa Maria 93456, 805/922-8313.

Danish Days, *September.* Contact Solvang Business Association.

■ *A LITTLE BACKGROUND*

Located on the outskirts of Los Angeles in Santa Barbara County, Solvang (meaning literally "sunny field" in Danish) is about a 4–5 hour drive from the Bay Area on Hwy 101. A replica of a Danish town, the business section features authentic architecture complete with thatched roofs and storks perched by the chimneys. Each year this tiny town has more than a million visitors.

Solvang is a popular destination for Christmas shopping, because there are more than 250 specialty shops offering a wide variety of giftwares—many imported from Europe. Seasonal decorations on the streets and in shop windows make for a festive mood. Most visitors make a stop at the **Jule Hus** (Christmas House), open throughout the year, to purchase Christmas decorations.

■ *ROUTE*

Located approximately 90 miles south of Morro Bay, 295 miles south of San Francisco. Take Hwy 1 to Hwy 101 to Hwy 246.

■ *WHERE TO STAY*

Dannebrog Inn, *1450 Mission Dr., 805/688-3210; $34–$40; indoor pool, color TV, continental breakfast included.*

King Frederik Motel, *1617 Copenhagen Dr., 805/688-5515, toll-free reservations 800/528-1234; $30–$32; pool, color TV, includes breakfast in room.*

Meadowlark Motel, *2644 Mission Dr. (1¼ miles east of town), 805/688-4631; $16–$26; pool, TV, putting green, some kitchens.*

Royal Copenhagen Motel, *1579 Mission Dr., 805/688-5561; $28–$36; pool, color TV, includes morning coffee and Danish at a nearby bakery.* Guests stay in rooms that are reproductions of actual Danish buildings.

Sanja Cota Motor Lodge, *3099 E. Hwy 246 (2½ miles east of town), Santa Ynez 93460, 805/688-5525; $19–$26; pool, color TV, includes morning coffee and Danish.*

■ *WHERE TO EAT IN TOWN*

The Belgian Cafe, *475 First St., 805/688-6316; daily 8am–4pm.* Outdoor dining is pleasant on a patio decorated with profusely blooming flowers. Gigantic freshly-baked Belgian waffles are served with a choice of toppings. Crepes, Danish sausage, homemade soups, and Solvang fruit wines round out the menu. Fresh strawberries are available year around.

Ellen's Danish Pancake House, *1531 Mission Dr., 805/688-5312; closed Tu.* Danish-style pancakes are the specialty of the house. Breakfast is served all day.

Hanne's Polsevogen, *436 Second St., 805/688-5595.* Danish hot dogs are dispensed from an authentic Danish hot dog wagon.

Wholly Cow! Restaurant, *Atterday/Mission St., 805/688-6861; daily 10am–10pm.* Hamburgers, homemade potato chips, wilted spinach salad, and ice cream treats are just a few of the foods available here.

■ *WHERE TO EAT NEARBY*

Andersen's Pea Soup Restaurant, *Avenue of Flags, Buellton, 805/688-5581; daily 7am–midnight; highchairs, booster seats, children's portions.* A reproduction of a Swiss chalet, this famous restaurant offers delicious pea soup as well as homemade breads, thick creamy milkshakes, and other inexpensive foods. Though their pea soup factory is actually located in Stockton, the famous soup is the star of the menu. Children are given their own menus and a pea-green crayon when seated. This keeps them busy for at least ten seconds. After your meal you are treated to a complimentary wine and coffee tasting in the gift shop area. Outside the kids can ride mechanical horses, cars, etc. for one thin dime. The gift shop sells that famous canned pea soup as well as many other items. Colorful, free postcards are available at each table.

Valley Steak House, *405 E. Hwy 246, Buellton, 805/688-3415; daily 11:30am–2:30pm, 5–10:30pm.* This popular family spot is known for its large selection of meats, which are cooked-to-order on an oak wood barbecue pit.

■ *WHAT TO DO IN TOWN*

Bicycles. They may be rented in town and provide a good way to leisurely see the sights.

Miniature Golf. An 18-hole course is located across from Solvang Park.

Mission Santa Ines, *1760 Mission Dr.; M–Sat 9:30am–4:30pm, Sun noon–5pm; adults 50¢, under 16 free.* Featuring hand-painted murals and lovely gardens, this is the 19th in the chain of 21 California missions. Founded in 1804, it is now fully restored. Recorded tours are available.

Ride the Honen (hen); *adults 75¢, children 50¢.* Tour the town on a Danish streetcar pulled by two horses. Guided tours begin at Solvang Park.

■ *WHAT TO DO NEARBY*

Ballard School, *in Ballard.* Built in 1883, this one-room little red

schoolhouse now is a good spot to picnic.

Lompoc, *south on Hwy 246 to junction of Hwy 1.* Over half the world's flower seed is grown in this valley. Spring and summer provides a stunning show of color. A Flower Festival is held here each June.

Mission La Purisima State Historical Park, *west on Hwy 246; daily 8am–5pm; 25¢.* Located on 1,000 acres, this mission is completely restored and provides and accurate picture of what life was like in the mission over 150 years ago. It is the best preserved of the 21 missions.

Nojoqui Falls Park, *6½ miles south of Solvang; free.* Scattered over this 60-acre park you will find a waterfall, swings, slides, horseshoe pits, an athletic field, picnic and barbecue facilities, and trails.

COAST NORTH

Redwood Empire Association
360 Post St., Suite 401
San Francisco 94108
415/421-6554
For an informative "Visitor's Guide" to the counties
north of San Francisco, send $1 to the above address—
or pick it up in person free. Over 300 brochures are also
available. Hours are M–F 9am–5pm.

■ *A WORD OF CAUTION*
The rocky cliffs and beaches along the coast are scenically
beautiful. In our appreciation of the beauty, we sometimes
forget that they are also dangerous. Standing at the edge of
a cliff with the surf pounding around your feet is tempting,
but it is also dangerous. People have been washed out to sea
that way. Don't be one of them. Be careful. Stay on trails.
Obey posted signs. And take special care not to let your children run loose.

HIGHWAY 1 LODGING

■ *ROUTE*
Begins approximately 90 miles north of San Francisco. Take
Hwy 101 to Hwy 1.

STRONG BACKWASH
SLEEPER WAVES
RIP CURRENTS

DANGER

SURF
UNSAFE
NO
LIFEGUARD

■ *WHERE TO STAY*

Bodega Bay, George Haig Realty, *P.O. Box 38, Bodega Bay 94923,*
707/875-3503. Bodega Bay lodging ranging from cozy cottages to
luxurious homes may be rented through this resource.

Chanslor Ranch, *P.O. Box 327, Bodega Bay 94923, 707/875-3386; $19–*
$22 per person, special rates for children; special bunkhouse accom-
modates a party of up to ten people; dining facilities. Pack up the

kids and move 'em out to the Chanslor Ranch, a 700-acre working cattle ranch located in Bodega Bay. Hearty breakfasts and family-style dinners are served in the Ranchhouse dining room. Wind-down activities include horseback riding, hiking, fishing, golfing, and local sightseeing—or you can help milk a cow.

THE SEA RANCH

Homes: *Rams Head Realty, P.O. Box 123, The Sea Ranch 95497, 707/785-2427; $85–$170/two nights; two night minimum.* Staying in an award-winning vacation home and enjoying the beauty of the wind-swept coastal scenery are two compelling reasons to visit The Sea Ranch. A bar and restaurant are located in the nearby Lodge, and guests may enjoy the use of swimming pools, tennis courts, saunas, hiking trails, and a children's playground. Horse rentals and a golf course are available at extra charge.

Lodge: *P.O. Box 44, The Sea Ranch 95497, 707/785-2371; $40–$60; cribs, some fireplaces, same facilities as mentioned above.*

Mar Vista Cottages, *35101 Hwy 1, Anchor Bay, Gualala 95445, 707/884-3522; $33–$44; cribs, ocean views, kitchens, playground.* Located in the "banana belt," these cottages are just a short walk from a sandy beach with a gentle surf. Guests enjoy two lakes complete with ducks, children's play equipment and sand boxes, and a barbecue area.

Serenisea, *36100 Hwy 1 south, Gualala 95445, 707/884-3836; $30–$60; kitchens, fireplaces.* Only four cabins are available at this tiny resort located on 2½ acres of coastal land. Two have extraordinary ocean views, and one is a luxury cabin complete with sauna, stereo, and sundeck. This is a good spot for whale watching and tidepooling. Skindiving, rock fishing, and swimming may be enjoyed nearby.

MENDOCINO

■ *A LITTLE BACKGROUND*

For a rejuvenating, quiet escape from the hectic pace of city life, pack up your car and head for Mendocino. Now a historic monument, this tiny artists' colony is built in a pastel Cape Cod-style of architecture and exudes the feeling that it belongs to a time past. To really slow down your system, consider parking your car and not using it for the duration of your visit. You can get anywhere in town with a short walk.

Keep in mind that Mendocino has a limited water supply, and be careful not to waste. Also, be aware that there is a Volunteer Fire Department, and its alarm may go off in the middle of the night. Resembling the scream of an air raid siren, it can be quite startling—even if you are aware what it is.

The night life here is of the early-to-bed-early-to-rise variety. My family's agenda usually includes dinner out, a stroll through town, a drink at the Mendocino Hotel or Sea Gull Inn, possibly a movie at the Art Center, and then off to bed.

Be sure to make your lodging reservations a few weeks in advance; in-town lodging is limited.

■ *ROUTE*

Located approximately 140 miles north of San Francisco. Take Hwy 101 to Hwy 1 or Hwy 101 to Hwy 128 west to Hwy 1.

■ *STOPS ALONG THE WAY*

On your drive to Mendocino, a picnic makes a good choice for a lunch stop. A good picnic area is near the **Geyser Peak Winery** (707/433-5349), located a mile north of Geyserville (take Canyon Rd. exit). There you will find picnic tables, barbecue facilities, and a self-guided nature trail. Countless more picnic spots may be found along Hwy 128. Several stores on this highway carry picnic supplies. In the summer and fall, apples and apple cider may be purchased at roadside stands found sprinkled along the way. On Hwy 1, about ten miles north of Fort Ross, **Salt Point State Park** has picnic tables and a beach access.

If you prefer to stop at a restaurant, there are several good ones en route. On Hwy 101 try the restaurant at the **Souverain Winery** (707/857-3789). An elegant luncheon is available daily except Monday. Highchairs and booster seats are available and children are welcome, but you'll want to be dressed up for this stop. You might prefer to bring your own picnic lunch and purchase a bottle of their wine to enjoy in the winery's picnic area. To reach the winery take the Independence Lane exit in Geyserville.

On Hwy 1 try the **River's End Restaurant** in Jenner. The food is fresh and unusual (terrine of rabbit and duckling with pistachios and lingonberry sauce, fish and chips with sauce remoulade, baked lamb moussaka), and the view is spectacular. A late lunch may be enjoyed at the **Greenwood Pier Cafe** in Elk. Inexpensive, casual, and popular with families, its menu features such temptations as homemade bread, fresh fruit, hot chocolate made with milk, fresh squeezed orange juice, scones, and quiche.

■ *WHERE TO STAY IN TOWN*

MacCallum House, *740 Albion St. (P.O. Box 206), 707/937-0289; $34.50–$54.50; cribs, dining facilities, continental breakfast included, two night minimum on weekends.* Charmingly decorated rooms are filled with antiques in this visually stunning 97-year-old house. Several cottages and a converted barn provide additional lodging. You can arrange to have a wine and cheese picnic basket packed for an outing.

Mendocino Coast Holiday Reservations, *P.O. Box 1143, 95460, 707/937-5033; $35–$75.* This personalized referral service can arrange for you to rent private homes and cottages on the Mendocino coast.

Mendocino Village Inn, *P.O. Box 626, 95460, 707/937-0246; $15–$33; cribs; some TV, views, fireplaces, and private bathrooms.* Built in 1882, this Victorian home is beautifully kept up. Known as "the house of the doctors" because it was originally built by a doctor and then bought in turn by three other doctors, it is now a cozy charming inn. The rooms are all different and decorated in an old-fashioned style.

Sea Gull Inn, *P.O. Box 317, 95460, 707/937-5204; $25; all rooms have private baths and electric blankets.*

Sea Rock Motel, *11101 N. Lansing St. (P.O. Box 286), 707/937-5517; $23–$44; most rooms have ocean views and fireplaces; some kitchens.* Located a quarter-mile from Mendocino's Main Street, this motel is made up mostly of individual cottages. Guests have access to a private cove and beach.

■ WHERE TO STAY NEARBY

Little River Inn, *Hwy 1, Little River 95456, 707/937-5942; $24–$80; golf course, dining facilities, breakfast included, beach accessible by footpath; some fireplaces and kitchens; two night minimum on weekends.* Built in 1853, this house became an inn in 1929 and now offers a choice of cottages, cozy attic rooms, and standard motel units—all of which offer garden or sea views. Take your pick. A western bar and dining room are also on the premises.

■ WHERE TO EAT

Cafe Beaujolais, *961 Ukiah, 707/937-5614; daily 7:30am–2pm, Sunday brunch 9am–2pm; highchairs.* Breakfast in this Victorian structure features the usual items along with such delights as fresh coffeecake, fruit salad with creme fraiche, and Mexican hot chocolate. Lunch changes daily and includes a variety of sandwiches, quiches, casseroles, soups, and salads.

Melody's Cookies, *630 Lansing St.* This teeny, tiny house is the home of huge, gigantic cookies. The kids are sure to love the cookies as well as the shop.

Mendocino Hotel, *Main St., 707/937-0511; daily 11:30am–2:30pm, 5:30–9:30pm, Sunday brunch 10:30am–2:30pm; highchairs, booster seats, children's portions.* The most inexpensive way to enjoy the stained-glass and oriental carpet splendor here is to stop in for a fancy drink in the comfortable, sedate bar or a meal in the dining room, furnished in antique oak. Meals are in the medium price range. Lunch typically offers such items as Mexican flautas, oyster loaf, and a special sandwich. Dinner entrees include abalone steak, crab and artichoke casserole, veal piccata, and prime rib.

Sea Gull Inn, *Lansing/Ukiah Sts., 707/937-5204; daily 7:30am–9pm; children's portions.* Recovered now from a devastating fire, the Sea Gull is again offering fine food and drink; the lodging facilities, undamaged in the fire, are the same as always. The restaurant looks much as it used to, but the bar has changed dramatically. Formerly located downstairs, it was cozy and cramped and had a harem-tent decor. Now it is upstairs with an airy, noisy, spacious, woodsy feeling. It seems to be even more popular than before. Though no minors are allowed after 10pm, until then children attend in large numbers and seem to have as much fun as the adults. Maybe they feel at home because of the nursery rhyme illustrations decorating the ceilings: Jack and the Beanstalk (the giant looks suspiciously like Kris Kristofferson), the Princess and the Pea (not a commentary on the lodging),

and Rapunzel. When my family comes here, we adapt to our "tourist" status and just sit back with an Irish Coffee and watch the locals carry on.

Village Deli, *Main St., 707/937-5827; daily 10:30am–6pm.* The usual delicatessen items are available here, along with some very tasty homemade items. This makes a good stop for an inexpensive meal or to fill your picnic basket.

■ *WHAT TO DO*

For a current listing of local events, check the postings in the entryway to the Sea Gull restaurant.

- Take the little path behind the church on Main Street down to the beach to do some **Beachcombing.**
- Make a **Kelp Horn.** Take a long, thin piece of fresh bull kelp. Cut off the bulb on the end and discard. Wash out the tube in the ocean so that it is hollow. Wrap it over your shoulder, and blow through the small end. The longer the tube, the greater the resonance.
- **Feed the Ducks** at the pond on Main Street.
- See a **Movie** at the **Mendocino Art Center.** They are usually shown on weekend evenings and admission is inexpensive. One summer there

was a charming schedule of silent movies accompanied by live piano music. Call 707/937-5818 for details. While you're calling, inquire about the schedule for the Sunday afternoon **Concerts** and **Plays.**

Catch a Canoe, *located off Hwy 1 at Comptche-Ukiah Rd. (P.O. Box 686), 707/937-0273; daily 9am–dusk; minimum $3/hour; reservations recommended.* Rent kayaks, row boats, canoes, and paddleboats here. A leisurely day's drifting down calm Big River will afford you opportunities to picnic in the wilderness and maybe even find your own private swimming hole. Call the shop for tide information and advice on when to start your trip.

Pygmy Forest, *located south of town on Airport Rd.* This forest is especially interesting because the leached soil produces miniature trees. The trail is 1/3 mile long and takes about 15 minutes to walk. A trail brochure, describing the various types of trees, is available at the trailhead.

FORT BRAGG

Fort Bragg Chamber of Commerce
P.O. Box 1141
(332 N. Main St.)
Fort Bragg 95437
707/964-3153

■ *WHERE TO STAY IN TOWN*

Beachcomber Motel, *21800 N. Hwy 1, 707/964-2402; $32–$35; cribs, TV, beach access, some kitchens and ocean views.*

The Grey Whale Inn, *615 N. Main St., 707/964-0640; $26.50–$42; rooftop sundeck, laundry facilities, lounge with pool table, some ocean views, continental breakfast included.* This unusual hotel was once a hospital.

Harbor Lite Lodge, *120 N. Harbor Dr., 707/964-0221; $30–$34; cribs, color TV, sauna, playground, some private balconies with harbor view.*

Hi-Seas Ocean View Motel, *21950 N. Hwy 1, 707/964-5929; $28–$30; cribs, private beach, all rooms have ocean views, some kitchens.*

Pine Beach Inn, *one mile south of Fort Bragg (P.O. Box 1173), 707/964-5603; $32–$42; cribs, color TV, dining facilities in summer, two tennis courts, some ocean views.* Located on 12 acres, this modern motel allows guests to relax and enjoy a private cove and beach.

■ *WHERE TO STAY NEARBY*

Emandal, *16500 Hearst Rd., Willits 95490, 707/459-5439; rates vary according to age, adults $187/week; August only; cribs, includes three meals per day.* Emandal is a 1,000-acre working cattle and pig ranch located on the Eel River about 16 miles northeast of Willits. A guest ranch since 1908, the farm grows the makings for the homecooked meals served here. Guests are housed in rustic, one-room cabins dating from 1916. Guests may hike, ride horses, and swim in the river. If you want to stay less than a week, weekdays offer your best chance for a shorter reservation.

Palace Hotel, *272 N. State St., Ukiah 95482, 707/468-9291, toll-free reservations 800/862-4698; $24–$65; cribs, dining facilities, continental breakfast included.* Built in 1891, the Palace Hotel was recently refurbished to its original plush splendor. It was once a stopover for stage travelers from the Bay Area on the way to Eureka, and it has hosted many famous people in the past. Now you can rest here and see famous people in the hotel's Back Door Club. The restaurant serves a gourmet menu daily at lunch and dinner and also at the weekend brunch. Highchairs and booster seats are available for children. While here, you can visit nearby wineries, a hot springs spa, and maybe take a raft trip.

■ *WHERE TO EAT*

Cap'n Flint's, *32250 N. Harbor Dr., Noyo, 707/964-9447; daily 11am–8:30pm; highchairs, children's portions.* It gets crowded here, so be prepared for a short wait. The reasonably-priced menu offers sandwiches, assorted varieties of fish and chips, shrimp wontons (a house specialty), and Louis salads.

Casa del Noyo, *500 Casa del Noyo Dr., 707/964-9991; W–M 6-9:30pm, closed Tu; highchairs, booster seats.* Located in a woodsy setting and featuring views of the inlet, this inn serves fresh fish, prime rib, and stuffed chicken breasts. A bar with fireplace is located in the cellar. Overnight accommodations are also available.

Egghead Omelettes, *326 N. Main St., 707/964-5005; F–Tu 8am–2pm, closed W & Th; booster seats.* This cheerful, popular, and tiny diner serves 40 varieties of huge omelettes. Regular breakfast items are also available, and at lunch sandwiches join the menu.

The Flying Bear, *356 N. Main St., 707/964-5671; M–Sat 10am–5:30pm, Sun noon–5:30pm.* Handmade candy and ice cream are featured here. They dip their own chocolate-covered creams, they make their own marshmallow for the rocky road, they roast their own almonds for the English Toffee, and they make the thick peanut brittle fresh each day. Preservatives are never used.

At Northspur, half-way to Willits on the Skunk Train Line.

Piedmont Hotel, *102 S. Main St., 707/964-2410; daily 11am–2pm, 5–9pm.* This noisy, popular spot serves family-style Italian dinners. Entree choices include seafood, chicken, and steak.

■ *WHAT TO DO*

Georgia-Pacific Nursery & Logging Museum, *90 W. Redwood Ave., 707/964-5651; nursery: M–F 9am–4pm April–November, museum: M–F 8am–5pm; free.* Stop in for a free look at four million trees. There is a visitor center, nature trails, and picnic tables. The logging museum is filled with historical photographs and mementos. When you get home, look in your mailbox for the free package of redwood seeds which is mailed to all visitors.

Mendocino Coast Botanical Gardens, *2 miles south of Fort Bragg on Hwy 1 (18220 N. Hwy 1), 707/964-4352; daily 8:30am–6pm; adults $2.50, 13–18 $1.50, 6–12 75¢, under 6 free.* Guided tours are available through these 47 acres of flowering plants. Picnic facilities are available as well as a restaurant and (plant) nursery. There are often weekend concerts scheduled in the summer. Call for details.

Skunk Train, *foot of Laurel St., 707/964-6371; adults $9.90 round trip, 5–11 $4.95, under 5 free if they don't occupy a seat; make reservations by contacting: California Western Railroad, P.O. Box 907, Fort Bragg 95437; train leaves at 9:45am and returns at 5pm.* For those of you with little skunks who love trains—voilà! The skunk train. The train gets its name from the fact that the original trains emitted unpleasant odors from their gas engines. They smelled not unlike skunks. Now a steam engine pulls the train in the summer (the Super Skunk) and a diesel engine is used the rest of the year (the Skunk). The ride takes you through 40 miles of dense redwood forest, over 31 bridges and trestles, and through two deep mountain tunnels. The 7½ hour round trip runs between Fort Bragg and Willits, where there is a stopover. There are several scheduling choices, so send for their informative brochure before you make your reservations.

Weller House Museum, *524 Stewart St., 707/964-3061; daily in summer 10am–5pm, weekends in winter by appointment; adults $1.25, under 12 50¢.* Listed on the National Register of Historic Places, the Weller House is a unique 1886 Victorian open for public touring. Antique toys and a spectacular redwood ballroom are just a few of the interesting things you'll see here.

EUREKA

Eureka Chamber of Commerce
2112 Broadway
Eureka 95501
707/442-3738

Guided tours of the town leave the Chamber of Commerce on Tuesdays and Thursdays at 9am. The charge is $8.50/person and includes lunch. Call for reservations.

■ *A LITTLE BACKGROUND*

The best of the remaining virgin redwoods are in this area's state parks, all of which were established in the 1920s. Ambitious logging activity has, over time, changed the scenery quite a bit.

The off season makes a good, if cold, time to visit the quiet northcoast redwood country around Humboldt Bay. Pack your warmest clothing, kiss the sunshine goodbye, and get

ready to enjoy the scenic, stunning beauty of this quiet, foggy, uncrowded area.

- **ROUTE**
Located approximately 285 miles north of San Francisco. Take Hwy 101 all the way.

- **WHERE TO STAY IN TOWN**
Carson House, *1209 4th St., 707/443-1601; $28–$38; pool, TV.*

Eureka Inn, *7th/F Sts., 707/442-6441; $36–$125; pool, TV, dining facilities.* The English Tudor Eureka Inn is *the* place to stay and will provide you with a free brochure outlining a walking tour of the town's Victorian homes.

Motel Row. Plenty of last-minute accommodations may usually be found by driving down Broadway and 4th Streets. Both streets are lined with motels.

- **WHERE TO STAY NEARBY**
Avenue of the Giants, *see page 77.*

Bishop Pine Lodge, *900 Patricks Point Dr., Trinidad 95570, 707/677-3314; $22–$27.* These rustic, secluded cottages are located in the redwoods. Forest and ocean trails are nearby.

California State University, Humboldt, *Arcata 95521, 707/826-3451; $14; summer only.* Stay in a campus dormitory. Accommodations are not luxurious, but the rates are certainly right and the novelty makes up for any inconvenience. Meals are available at a small additional cost.

Hartsook Inn Resort, *Hwy 101, Piercy 95467, 707/247-3305; $20–$32; dining facilities, closed Nov–March.* These cottages are located in a rustic redwood setting adjoining Richardson Grove State Park. Swimming in the river and lawn games are available.

Requa Inn, *Star Route 720, Klamath 95548, 707/482-5231; $41.50; dining facilities, breakfast included.* This is a historic hotel located at the mouth of the Klamath River.

■ WHERE TO EAT IN TOWN

Lazio's Seafood Restaurant, *at the foot of C St., 707/442-2337; daily 11am–10pm; children's portions.* Fresh seafood, caught by Lazio's own commercial fishing operation, is the specialty here. Picture windows allow diners to watch the fishermen bringing in the catch. It's always crowded and reservations are not taken, so expect a short wait.

McDonald's, *4th/S Sts., 707/442-8821; daily 6:30am–11pm.* This branch is worth pointing out, because live organ music may often be enjoyed along with your Big Mac and fries. Music hours are irregular, so call ahead if you want entertainment.

Old Town, *see page 77.*

Samoa Cookhouse, *(from Hwy 101 take Samoa Bridge to end, turn left on Samoa Rd., take first left turn), 707/442-1659; daily 7am–11am $2.95, 11am–2pm $2.85, 5–10pm $5.75, Sun 6am–noon and dinner noon–10pm, special prices for children, under 3 free; highchairs, booster seats.* The fare changes daily in this "last of the western cookhouses." There are no menu choices offered except for breakfast. Just sit down, and the food starts arriving while you rub elbows with some *real* lumberjacks—and, of course, some other tourists. Hearty, delicious family-style meals are served at long tables in the huge dining hall. A typical lunch might consist of marinated bean salad, soup, homemade bread, ham salad, mashed potatoes and gravy, barbecued ribs, mixed vegetables, coffee, and coconut pudding topped with whipped cream! A fantastic value! Everything is cooked fresh and served in generous portions. The only item not included in the flat price is milk. After dining you can wander through the mini-museum which is housed off one of the three large dining rooms. Freshly-baked loaves of bread and toy logging trucks are available for purchase and make appropriate souvenirs of your visit. A brisk walk along the nearby driftwood-strewn beach is enjoyable either before or after your feast. Several unmarked turnoffs lead from Samoa Rd. to the beach.

■ *WHERE TO EAT NEARBY*

Red Pepper, *856 10th St., Arcata, 707/822-2138; children's portions.*
This casual restaurant features Sonora-style Mexican food—mild and
rich in tomato flavoring.

■ *WHAT TO DO IN TOWN*

Carson Mansion, *2nd/M Sts.* This is said to be the most photographed
house in the United States and the "queen" of Victorian architecture.

Clarke Memorial Museum, *3rd/E Sts., 707/443-1947; Tu–Sat 10am–4pm,
closed Sun & M.* Here you'll see an outstanding collection of mounted
birds and bird eggs, China dolls, Indian artifacts, pioneer relics, and
historical photographs of the area.

Coast Oyster Co., *foot of A St., 707/442-2947; in winter M–F 9am–2pm.*
Take a self-guided tour of this oyster processing plant, located next
door to Lazio's Restaurant. Operating hours are irregular, so call for
current information.

Fort Humboldt State Historical Monument, *3431 Fort Ave., 707/443-
4588; daily 9am–6pm; free.* Exhibits include some locomotives, a
restored logger's cabin, and displays of pioneer logging methods. This
is a good spot for a picnic.

Humboldt Bay Harbor Cruise, *foot of C. St., 707/442-3738, 443-2714;
daily in summer at 1, 2:30, and 4pm; adults $3, 12–17 $2, 6–11 $1.50,*

Dolbeer steam donkey at Fort Humboldt.

under 6 free. The 75-minute cruise aboard the *M.V. Madakat*—which once ferried workers to the lumber mills across the bay in Samoa—allows you a sweeping view of the bay, its wildlife, and its bustling activity. The last boat out is a sunset cruise. Schedules vary considerably from year to year, so be sure to verify the current departure times.

Old Town, *1st/2nd/3rd Sts. from D to G Sts.* On a stroll through this waterfront area you will be treated to beautifully restored commercial and residential buildings. There are restaurants where you may enjoy a leisurely meal and interesting shops to browse in. **The Inside Track** (222 1st St., 707/442-7323) is a gift shop housed inside an old rail car. Reasonably-priced meals are available at **Tomaso's Tomato Pies** (216 E St., 707/445-0100; daily 8am–10pm), where you can get Sicilian-style pizza as well as spinach pie, calzone, spinzone, and submarine sandwiches, and **Fat Albert's** (312-316 E St., 707/443-8887; daily), where lunch offerings include hamburgers and sandwiches and dinner features steak, fish, and Italian items.

Sequoia Park and Zoo, *Glatt/W Sts., 707/443-7331; daily in summer 10am–7pm, in winter until 5pm; petting zoo open weekends noon–4pm; free.* The background for this combination zoo-playground-picnic area is a 52-acre grove of virgin redwoods. There are also trails and a duck pond.

▪ *WHAT TO DO NEARBY*

Alton and Pacific Railroad, *on Hwy 36 ½ mile east of Alton (Route 1, Box 477, Fortuna 95540); summer only Th–Tu 11am–5pm, closed W; adults $2, 3-15 $1.25, under 3 free.* Enjoy a ride on this two-foot narrow-gauge wood-burning steam train.

The Avenue of the Giants, *Humboldt Redwoods State Park, Weott, 707/946-2311; free.* The Avenue of the Giants, which is actually the old Hwy 101, begins a few miles north of Garberville near Phillipsville and continues on for approximately 40 miles to just south of the town of Pepperwood, where it rejoins the busy new Hwy 101. This breathtaking route parallels the freeway and the Eel River and takes you winding through grove after grove of huge redwoods. While you're driving this unique stretch of road, keep your eyes open for these special sights: near Myers Flat, **The Shrine Drive-thru Tree** with a circumference of approximately 64 feet; **The Children's Forest** (located across the south fork of the Eel River)—a 1,120-acre memorial to children; and **Williams Grove** with its picturesque picnic sites located on the Eel River (don't forget your swimsuits); near Weott, **Rockefeller Forest,** referred to by some as "the world's finest forest."

The "Avenue" has its own series of accommodations scattered throughout the route. It is quite inviting to see the charming cottages and swimming pools speckled with sunlight as you drive through this huge forest. A few of the best are:

Deerhorn Lodge, *Phillipsville, 707/943-3024*

Miranda Gardens Resort, *Miranda, 707/943-3011*

Whispering Pines Motel, *Miranda, 707/943-3160*

Squirrel Bus Tour, *P.O. Box 353, Garberville 95440, 707/986-7526; M, W, F, & Sat 10am June–Sept; adults $15, 2–12 $7.50.* Leave your car behind and take a seven-hour bus tour of the Avenue of the Giants (from Garberville to Scotia) and a redwood lumber mill. A shorter, less expensive tour is also available.

Confusion Hill, *Hwy 101, Piercy, 707/925-6456; daily 8:30am–7:30pm April–Sept; hill: adults $1.50, 6–12 75¢, under 6 free; train: adults $1.50, 6–12 75¢, under 6 free.* Take a pleasant train ride through a tree tunnel and to the crest of a hill in the redwoods. Then visit Confusion Hill, a spot where gravity appears to be defied and you'll see water run *up*hill and a 250 foot tree house.

Covered Bridges, *take Hwy 101 south to Elk River Rd., follow Elk River Rd. to either Bertas Rd. or Zane Rd.* These two all-wood covered bridges were constructed in 1936.

Demonstration Forests. To educate the public about their function, many lumber firms have set up self-guided tours through parts of their forests. These are also good spots to enjoy a picnic.

Louisiana Pacific Corporation, *on Hwy 1 one mile north of Rockport.*

Louisiana Pacific, Samoa Division, *on old Hwy 101 one mile north of Trinidad.*

Masonite Corporation, *on Hwy 128 west of Navarro.*

Pacific Lumber Company, *on Hwy 101 four miles south of Scotia.*

Rellim Redwood Company, *on Hwy 101 three miles south of Crescent City.*

Simpson Timber Company, *on Hwy 299 one mile east of Blue Lake.*

The Dollhouse Museum, *1710 Main St., Fortuna, 707/725-3738; daily 9am–6pm; adults 50¢, children 25¢.* Here you will see an interesting collection of antique dollhouses and furnishings.

Drive-through Tree, *Hwy 1, Leggett, 707/925-6363; daily 9am–6pm; $2/car.* Most average-size cars can squeeze through the hole in this 315 foot high, 21 foot diameter redwood tree. Bring your camera. Nature trails and lakeside picnic areas are available for the use of visitors.

Ferndale, *6 miles north of Scotia, 5 miles off Hwy 101.* This entire town is composed of restored Victorian buildings and is known as "Victorian Village." Located in farm country, the town has become somewhat of an artists' colony and is filled with antique shops, a few galleries and restaurants, and a great toy store.

Humboldt State University. Find out what's happening on campus (concerts, films, plays, and other activities) by calling 707/826-3928.

Klamath Jet-Boat Kruises, *located in Requa about 40 miles north on Hwy 101 (P.O. Box 5, Klamath 95548), 707/482-4191; adults $15, 4–11 $5, under 4 free; reservations advised in summer.* Take a six-hour, 64-mile cruise on the Klamath River. The trip begins at 9am, and a lunch stop is made at the Klamath Lodge.

Pacific Lumber Company, *on Hwy 101 27 miles south of Eureka, Scotia, 707/764-2222; M–F 10am–4pm, closed weekends; free.* Enjoy a self-guided tour through the world's largest redwood lumber mill. Get your pass for the hour tour in the old First National Bank building, now a logging museum. Scotia is one of the last company-owned lumber towns in the west and is built entirely of redwood.

Prairie Creek Redwoods State Park, *Hwy 101, Orick 95555, 707/488-2861; daily 9am–5pm; free.* The eight-mile gravel road to Gold Bluffs Beach and Fern Canyon takes you through a beautiful forest area on into an area with ferncovered cliffs. A refuge for one of the few remaining herds of native Roosevelt elk, this area tends to be foggy and cold.

Redwood National Park, *Orick.*

Inner Tube Float Trips, *707/464-6101.* These rides on the Smith River are especially good for children. Call for further information and reservations.

Shuttle Bus to Tall Trees Grove, *707/488-3461; daily in summer 9am–4pm; adults $1, under 12 25¢.* This bus takes people to within a mile of the Tall Trees Grove, which contains the world's tallest tree (367.8 feet) as well as the third and sixth tallest trees. It is a two-mile round-trip walk from the dropoff point.

WINE COUNTRY

SONOMA AREA

Sonoma Valley Chamber of Commerce
453 First St. East
Sonoma 95476
707/996-1033

- *A LITTLE BACKGROUND*

    Toddlers can be difficult on a winery tour. Out of courtesy
    for the other tour participants (a noisy child interferes with
    the guide's presentation), you might consider selecting a mem-
    ber of your party to stay with the child while the rest go on
    the tour. Most wineries allow you to taste wines without go-
    ing on the tour; so if it is *one of those days* with your little
    ones, sample a few wines and things may suddenly seem better.

    Bring along a bottle of grape juice and some plastic wine
    glasses so that the children can "taste" too (my children call
    this "baby wine").

    Many wineries have adjoining picnic areas. An ideal agenda
    is to tour a winery, taste, and then buy a bottle of the wine
    you enjoyed most to drink with your prepacked picnic lunch.
    A picnic will allow children time to romp while the adults
    relax.

Because the wine country is so close to the Bay Area, this trip can easily be made into a one-day adventure. For a free booklet, "California's Wine Wonderland," send a stamped self-addressed legal size envelope to: California Wine Institute, 165 Post St., San Francisco 94108.

- ### ROUTE
Located approximately 45 miles north of San Francisco. Take Hwy 101 to Hwy 37 to Hwy 121 to Hwy 12.

- ### WHERE TO STAY
El Pueblo Motel, *896 W. Napa St., 707/996-3651, 996-3652; cribs, pool, TV; $22–$40.*

- ### WHERE TO EAT
Au Relais, *691 Broadway, 707/996-1031; W–M lunch and dinner, closed Tu; highchairs; reservations essential.* How many fine French restaurants do you know of where you can take the kids? Au Relais, meaning literally "a place to rest," usually features a boisterous atmosphere and is reminiscent of a French country inn. Tables are set closely together inside this converted house; outside on the flower-bedecked patio there is a little more elbow room. Dinner entrees include cassoulet maison (a casserole with lamb, pork, bacon, garlic sausage, duck, white beans, and tomato), poached salmon with shrimp sauce, and a daily special. I doubt the kids will appreciate the escargots appetizer. Desserts include chocolate truffle cake, mocha mousse, and cafe filtre. The lunch menu is similar but less expensive and also offers crepes, sandwiches, and omelettes.

Eldorado on the Plaza, *405 First St., 707/996-3030; F–Tu 8:30am–10pm, closed W & Th; children's portions; reservations advised.* Enjoy Italian and American entrees while dining in this historic building.

For **Picnic Fare** you will want to stop at one of these shops to pick up provisions:

Old Sonoma Cremery, *First St./E. Spain, 707/938-2938; daily 9am–6pm.* Delicatessen items and made-to-order sandwiches are quickly available here. On the other side of the store, past the two-story waterfall, there is more seating and an ice cream concession.

Sonoma Cheese Factory, *2 Spain St., 707/996-2300; daily 9am–6pm.* This crowded shop stocks 101 types of cheese (including their famous Sonoma Jack made from a family recipe), cold cuts, salads, delicious marinated artichoke hearts, and cheesecake flown in from New Jersey. Sandwiches are made-to-order. If you wish to eat here, there are tables inside the shop as well as on the patio.

Sonoma French Bakery, *468 First St. East, 707/996-2691; W–Sat 8am–6pm, Sun 7:30am–noon, closed last two weeks of August.* This famous bakery makes sourdough French bread which is so delicious that people are willing to wait in line to purchase it. Flutes, rolls, croissants, gateau Basque bread, French and Danish pastries, and chocolantines are just a few of the other delights available.

■ WHAT TO DO IN TOWN

Depot Park Museum, *First St. West, 707/938-9765; W–Sun 1–4:30pm; adults 50¢, children 25¢.* This museum is housed in the restored North West Pacific Railroad Station.

Sonoma State Historic Park, *Spain/First St., 707/938-4779; daily 10am–5pm; adults 50¢, under 18 free.* Visitors here may inspect old adobe buildings from California's early days. Included are General Vallejo's city house and gardens, a two-story barracks, the Toscano Hotel, and the Mission San Francisco Solano, the last of the 21 missions to be built and now housing the noted collection of California mission paintings done by Jorgensen.

Sonoma Town Square Park. This old-fashioned park is great for picnics and letting the kids play off their energy. Adults will enjoy browsing in the various shops lining the square while the children frolic at the playground and feed the ducks in the tiny pond.

Train Town, *Hwy 12 south of Sonoma (P.O. Box 656), 707/938-3912; daily in summer 11am–5:30pm, weekends rest of year; adults $2, children $1.25.* The 15-minute ride on the Sonoma Gaslight and Western Railroad steam locomotive winds through ten acres of well-maintained grounds. Passengers see forests, a mountain, a lake, a 70 foot double truss bridge, a 50 foot steel girder bridge, a tunnel, and an aviary. A three-minute stop occurs in Lakeville, a miniature one-quarter size reproduction of an old mining town. The train takes on more water here, while the engineer distributes food for the kids to feed to the ducks and swans—the sole inhabitants of Lakeville.

■ WINERIES

Buena Vista Winery, *Old Winery Rd., 707/938-8504; daily 10am–5pm; free.* Picnic tables encircle the vine-covered entrance to this historic winery, now a state historical landmark. The picnic area is shaded by stately old eucalyptus trees growing on the banks of a tiny brook. Children can play in the courtyard adjacent to the picnic area. Do be careful with the bees, though, as my own child was once painfully stung while we adults were busy enjoying our wine. The winery offers a self-guided tour through its limestone cellars (the first in California) and winetasting in its casual, noisy tasting room. If you forget picnic supplies, Sonoma Cheese Factory sandwiches are available for purchase in the tasting room. This is the perfect spot for a memorable picnic.

Hacienda Wine Cellars, *1000 Vineyard Lane, 707/938-3220; daily 10am–5pm.* First visit the tasting room and sample some of the fine wines produced here. Then pick a bottle of your favorite to purchase for your picnic. Have it corked, and wander outside to the scenic picnic area. Wine glasses may be borrowed from the tasting room. Reservations may be made in advance for space in the relatively small picnic area, but usually there is plenty of room. Don't forget to bring along extra provisions to feed the ducks and geese that often wander up from the nearby pond.

Sebastiani Vineyards, *389 E. Fourth St., 707/938-5532; tours daily 10am–5pm; free.* After taking the interesting guided tour (one leaves every 20 minutes), a special treat of grape juice is awaiting the children in the tasting room. Isn't that thoughtful? Children are usually left out in wineries when it comes tasting time. In addition to housing America's largest collection of carved oak wine casks, this winery also has a museum of Indian artifacts which features a collection of over 1,000 arrowheads. Before you leave you may want to sign up for the interesting and free wine newsletter which is mailed out monthly.

■ *WHAT TO DO NEARBY*

Aero-Sport, *at the airport off Hwy 121 two miles north of Sears Point Raceway, Schellville, 707/938-2444; weekends 9am–5pm, weekdays by appointment; $25/scenic ride with one loop and one roll, $35/ full aerobatic ride.* Chuck Hunter takes riders on a 15–20 minute flight in his Stearman plane, once used to train World War II combat pilots. Call for an appointment. Depending upon size, children about age seven and over may also go along for the rides. Have your picnic *after* this excursion. Old and antique planes may be viewed at the airport.

Agua Caliente Mineral Springs and Swimming Pool, *17310 Vailette, Fetters Hot Springs, 707/996-6822; W–Sun in summer 10:30am–6pm, closed M & Tu, hours and days fluctuate so call before going; adults $3–$4, under 11 $1.50–$2.* One of the three pools here is filled from a 96° spring, one has unheated water, and one is a special children's pool. Picnic and barbecue facilities are available.

Jack London State Park, *off Hwy 12 in Glen Ellen, 707/938-5216; daily 10am–5pm; $1.50/car.* Though there are no tables, the spacious grounds here provide ample room for picnicking and romping. The oak-covered knoll at the entrance to the park is a choice spot to lay your blanket. Located in the Valley of the Moon, the park contains

Ruins of Wolf House, Jack London State Historic Park.

the ruins of Jack London's dream castle "Wolf House" and a museum built in his memory by his widow. The park, a gift of London's nephew, is the focus of pilgrimages by London devotees. To get yourself in the mood for this trek you may want to read a few London classics such as *The Call of the Wild* or *Martin Eden.*

Morton's Warm Springs, *1651 Warm Springs Rd. (located about seven miles north of town), Kenwood 95452, 707/833-5511; in summer Tu–Sun 10am–6pm, closed M and Oct–Apr; adults $1.75–$2.75, 2–11 $1.25, under 2 free.* Two large pools and one toddler wading pool allow everyone in the family to enjoy a refreshing swim. Lifeguards are on duty. There are picnic tables and barbecue pits as well as a large grassy area where you may sunbathe. Dressing rooms are available with free lockers. Teenagers seem to especially enjoy the recreation room with a juke box, ping pong tables, and pinball machines. A snack bar dispenses inexpensive sandwiches, soft drinks, and ice cream. A few rules: all drinks must be in cans —no glass containers allowed; no cutoffs are allowed to be worn in the pools.

ST. HELENA AREA

St. Helena Chamber of Commerce
1080 Main St.
St. Helena 94574
707/963-4456

■ *ROUTE*

Located approximately 70 miles north of San Francisco. Take
Hwy 101 to Hwy 37 to Hwy 121 to Hwy 29.

■ *WHERE TO STAY*

Burgundy House, *6711 Washington St., Yountville 94599, 707/944-2855; $48; Victorian crib, buffet breakfast included.* Though the
rooms in the main inn are inappropriate for families, there are three
cottages which offer family comfort. Each has two bedrooms and a
sitting room, bath, fireplace, kitchen, and yard. The stone walls of
this former brandy distillery are 22 inches thick.

El Bonita Motel, *195 Main St., St. Helena, 707/963-3216; $24–$40;
TV, pool.*

Harvest Inn, *One Main St., St. Helena; 707/963-WINE; $50–$75; color
TV, pool, jacuzzi, some fireplaces.* Nestled on a 21-acre working vineyard, this English Tudor-style inn offers antique furnishings and the
invitation to "stay with us and listen to the grapes grow."

Napa Valley Lodge, *Hwy 29 (P.O. Box L), Yountville, 707/944-2468,
toll-free reservations 800/528-1234; $46–$48; color TV, playground,
refrigerators, pool, whirlpool, private balconies with view of vineyard, some fireplaces.*

■ *WHERE TO EAT*

Beaulieu Vineyards, *see page 88.*

Maggie Gin's, *1234 Main St., St. Helena, 707/963-9764; Tu–Sat 11:30am–
2:30pm, 5–8:30pm, closed Sun & M; booster seats.* The menu here
is not extensive, but what is available is fresh, tasty, and prepared
without MSG. The Szechwan salad and ice creams (lychee, ginger,
or mango ice) are my personal favorites.

Mama Nina's, *6772 Washington St., Yountville, 707/944-2112; Th–Tu
5–10pm, closed W; children's portions; reservations suggested.* You
can order a la carte or complete dinners of the homemade pastas at
Mama Nina's. The tortellini Nina (small circles of pasta filled with
ground veal, parmesan cheese, and spices and topped with a delicate
sauce of cream, butter, finely minced chicken breast, and parmesan

cheese) is highly recommended. Gnocchi, tagliarini pesto, and fettucine Alfredo are available along with scampi and veal piccata. There are daily dessert specials as well as "sandpie" (an oatmeal cookie crust filled with vanilla ice cream and topped with hot fudge sauce and chopped peanuts), a mudpie (a chocolate cookie crust filled with coffee ice cream and topped with hot fudge sauce), and rum-raisin ice cream.

Oakville Grocery, *7856 St. Helena Hwy, Oakville, 707/944-8802; M–F 8am–6pm, Sat & Sun 10am–5pm.* Choose from a large selection of mustards, imported beers, mineral waters, natural juices, cheeses, and other deli items.

Napa Valley Olive Oil Manufactory, *835 McCorkle Ave./Charter Oak, St. Helena, 707/963-4173; daily 8am–6:30pm.* In addition to an unusual cold press olive oil, you can purchase bulk cheese, sausage, olives, and cracked walnuts. Sandwiches and cold drinks are not available. There is a picnic area outside.

VINTAGE 1870, *Washington St., Yountville:*

> **Chutney Kitchen,** *707/944-2788; M–F noon–3pm, weekends 11:30am–3:30pm; highchairs, children's portions.* Enjoy freshly prepared sandwiches and salads either inside or out on the cooling patio.

> **Court of Two Sisters;** *open daily.* Fancy pastries, tiny quiches, and people cookies are just a few of the delicious baked goods you'll find in this well-known bakery.

> **Kitchen Store Deli;** *daily 10am–5pm.* Basic picnic supplies are available here.

> **Vintage Cafe,** *707/944-2614; M–Th 10am–5pm, F–Sun 10am–6pm; highchairs.* Order your sandwich or tasty hamburger at the counter, and then enjoy it either inside or outside on the patio.

> **Vintage Sweet Shoppe;** *daily 10am–5pm.* Ice cream concoctions and a wide variety of candy are available in an old-time soda parlor atmosphere.

> **The Wurst Place,** *707/944-2224; Tu–Sun 10am–5pm.* Freshly-made sausage without nitrates, Boudin Blanc (chicken sausage), sauerkraut, pork chops, and specialty items like caul fat are available at this tiny shop.

V. Sattui, *see page 89.*

■ *WHAT TO DO*

Adventures Aloft, *6525 Washington St., Yountville 94599, 707/255-8688; weekdays $75/person, weekends $85/person.* Tour the Napa Valley via hot air balloon. You will spend about one hour in the air;

altitude and distance depend on which way the wind is blowing. After your scenic ride, you will receive a champagne toast. Children must be age three or older.

Lake Berryessa, *take Hwy 128 east from St. Helena.* This lake is over 25 miles long, 3 miles wide, and has an extensive shoreline. You can rent boats and waterskis, and the swimming is excellent—not to mention the fishing.

Old Bale Mill, *Hwy 29, St. Helena; daily 10am–4:30pm; free.* A well-preserved historic landmark, this grist mill was built in 1846. Seeing the 45 foot high water wheel allows for some exploring. The state is in the process of restoring it to full operation and plans to sell the resulting flour as souvenirs to visitors.

Silverado Museum, *1490 Library Lane, St. Helena, 707/963-3757; Tu-Sun noon–4pm, closed M; free.* Located in "The Hatchery," a stone building dating from 1884, this library houses over 7,000 pieces of Robert Louis Stevenson memorabilia. I suggest a family read-in of *A Child's Garden of Verses* and/or *Treasure Island* before or after this visit.

St. Helena Town Park, *Hwy 29/Adams, St. Helena.* There are picnic tables and a children's play area in this old-fashioned park.

Vintage 1870, *Washington St., Yountville.* Thirty-three shops—including a well-stocked toy store, a shop specializing in chutney preserves, and a kitchen store filled with cooking accessories—are housed inside this lovely old brick building which was formerly a winery. The Napa Valley Theatre Co. (707/944-8925) puts on summer performances in the theatre here. Outside is a play area and climbing structure. Sometimes you can see hot air balloons preparing for takeoff nearby.

Vintage Rail Shops. Adjacent to Vintage 1890, these shops are located inside old train cars.

■ WINERIES

Beaulieu Vineyards, *Hwy 29/Hwy 128, Rutherford; daily 10am–4pm.* Tired parents have a place to sit here while they taste wines. A film is shown periodically. The adjacent **Garden Restaurant** serves lunch daily in its outdoor patio, while the **Cottage Restaurant** dispenses fast food items. Neither of these restaurants are affiliated with Beaulieu.

Beringer/Los Hermanos Vineyards, *2000 Main St., St. Helena, 707/963-7115; tours daily 9:30am–3:45pm.* The Visitor's Center is based in the Rhine House—a beautiful oak-paneled, stained-glass-laden reproduction of a nineteenth century German house. Unfortunately, picnicking is not permitted on the beautifully landscaped grounds.

Christian Brothers, *Hwy 29, St. Helena, 707/963-2719; tours daily*

10:30am–4:30pm. Located in a beautiful, old stone building, this winery additionally features a lovely picnic area.

V. Sattui/St. Helena Cheese Factory, *Hwy 29, Oakville, 707/963-7774; daily in summer.* Taste wine while you purchase picnic supplies to enjoy outside in the spacious picnic area.

CALISTOGA

Calistoga Chamber of Commerce
1139 Lincoln Ave.
Calistoga 94515
707/942-6333

- **A LITTLE BACKGROUND**
  Calistoga, often called "the Hot Springs of the West," is enjoying a renaissance as a popular weekend and summer retreat. The name originated from a combination of *Cali*fornia and *Sara*toga (a New York spa). For a little more history, I suggest you read *The Silverado Squatters* by Robert Louis Stevenson. The town sits on top of a hot underground river and features many unpretentious spas—all geared to helping visitors relax, unwind, and get healthy in their pools filled from hot springs. Most offer services such as mud baths (the curative volcanic ash comes from Mount St. Helena), steam baths, and massages. Contact the place you're interested in to find out treatment details and prices. For a small fee, most of the mineral pools are available for day use by patrons who are not spending the night.

- **ROUTE**
  Located approximately 80 miles north of San Francisco. Take Hwy 101 to Hwy 37 to Hwy 121 to Hwy 29.

- **WHERE TO STAY**
  Calistoga Spa, *1006 Washington, 707/942-6269; $30–$32; color TV, some kitchens, includes use of pools; two night minimum on weekends; day use 105° covered jacuzzi and 100° mineral pool: adults $3.50, 18 and under $2.50, May–Sept; 85° Roman olympic outdoor pool: adults $2.50, 18 and under $1.50, May–Sept; mud baths, mineral baths, steam baths, and massage also available.*

Dr. Wilkinson's Hot Springs, *1507 Lincoln, 707/942-4102; $28–$38; color TV, cribs, some cottages and kitchens; pool use $4.* The Wilkinson family operates this pleasant spa. There is a hot mineral water pool with a view of the nearby mountains. And you won't want to miss taking a mud bath, consisting of white volcanic ash powder mixed with naturally heated mineral water. After 15 minutes of nude immersion, the bather takes a mineral bath, a steam bath, and then—swaddled in dry blankets—rests and cools. Ahhh! Massage is also available.

Pacheteau's Original Calistoga Hot Springs, *1712 Lincoln, 707/942-5589; $28; TV, kitchens, closed during Dec; 90° geyser mineral water swimming pool: adults $3, under 12 $2, daily 10am–6pm Apr–Oct.* The main attraction here is the pool; children especially seem to love it. The accommodations are duplex apartments with 1930s kitchens and bathrooms with piped in hot sulphur water. Mud baths are also available here.

Triple S Ranch, *4600 Mt. Home Ranch Rd., 707/942-6730; $14; pool, dining facilities, cabins.*

■ *WHERE TO CAMP*

Bothe-Napa Valley State Park, *see page 91.*

Calistoga Ranch Campground, *570 Lommel Rd., 707/942-6565.* A private lake for fishing, hiking trails, and an olympic-size swimming pool are located on the 167 acres of this rustic camping spot.

■ *WHERE TO EAT*

Matt's Steak House, *Hwy 128/Petrified Forest Rd., 707/942-5646; daily 11:45am–8:30pm.* Hamburgers, fried chicken, steaks, and barbecued ribs are available to enjoy inside, out on the patio, or to go.

Royal Fellowship Inn, *1880 Lincoln Ave., 707/942-4636; Th–M 5pm, closed Tu & W; children's portions.* The international menu of vegetarian meals changes daily and includes such items as teriyaki mushrooms, stuffed grape leaves with lemon sauce, and sukiyaki vegetables. Call for the current menu.

Silverado Restaurant, *1374 Lincoln, 707/942-6725; daily 7am–midnight; highchairs, booster seats.* Lots of comfortable booths and views of the sidewalk parade combine with the fresh and tasty food to make the Silverado a choice spot to dine. Hamburgers, sandwiches, omelettes, and homemade soups and desserts are available for lunch along with a choice of 23! non-alcoholic drinks and five alcoholic fruit daiquiris (peach, strawberry, banana, blueberry, pineapple).

■ *WHAT TO DO*

Bothe-Napa Valley State Park, *3601 Hwy 29 North, Calistoga 94515, 707/942-4575; $1.50/car.* You can picnic, hike, swim in the pool, and camp on the 1,242 acres that comprise this lovely park.

Calistoga Soaring Center, *1546 Lincoln, 707/942-5592; $27/person, $38/2 people, 2 and under free.* This 20-minute sightseeing trip in a glider covers up to ten miles and reaches altitudes of up to 2,500 feet and speeds of up to 70 mph.

Old Faithful Geyser, *1299 Tubbs Lane, 707/942-6463; daily 8am–sundown; adults $1.50, 6–13 75¢, under 6 free.* One of only three geysers that merit the name "Old Faithful," this geyser erupts every 40 minutes and shoots 350° water over 60 feet high. The show lasts 3–4 minutes. Picnic tables are available. By the way, the other two are at Yellowstone National Park and in New Zealand.

Petrified Forest, *five miles west of town on Petrified Forest Rd., 707/942-6667; daily 9am–6pm; adults $2, under 10 free.* Enjoy a leisurely ¼-mile stroll on a lovely self-guided path through this unusual forest. There is a small museum as well as picnic tables.

Pioneer Park, *1300 block of Cedar.* This is a pleasant park with a nice playground.

Pope Valley Parachute Center, *1996 Pope Canyon Rd., Pope Valley 94567,*

707/965-3400; $75/lesson. Skydiving lessons are given at 10am every Saturday morning. You may just watch. Call ahead to verify times.

Sharpsteen Museum and Sam Brannan Cottage, *1311 Washington St., 707/942-5911; weekends noon–4pm.* This museum and the adjacent Sam Brannan Cottage give visitors some pioneer history.

Bike Rentals, *Hauschildt's Ice Cream Parlor, 1255 Lincoln, 707/942-9923; daily noon–8pm; $1.50–$5/hour.* Choose from regular bikes, a three-wheeler with bucket seats and a canopy, two and four seat tandems, and side by sides. Baby carriers are available.

- ## WINERIES

Sterling Vineyards, *1111 Dunaweal Lane, 707/942-5151; daily 10:30am–4:30pm, in winter closed M & Tu; adults $2.50, under 16 free.* Accessible only by special gondola cars, the Sterling Winery was built to resemble a Greek monastery. Located on top of a hill, it features a stunning and unusual white stucco, cubist architecture. Wine tasting occurs outdoors on a terrace; visitors are served at tables. There is a self-guided tour. The gondola ride takes three minutes. If you are afraid of heights, call ahead to arrange to be driven up. Each adult is given a $2 credit toward purchase of Sterling Wines, available only at the vineyard.

CLEAR LAKE

Lake County Chamber of Commerce
P.O. Box 517
(875 Lakeport Blvd.)
Lakeport 95453
707/263-6131

- ## SPECIAL EVENTS

Lake County Fair, *Labor Day weekend.* Contact Chamber of Commerce for information.

Bass Tournament, *annual.* Contact Chamber of Commerce for information.

- ## A LITTLE BACKGROUND

From the 1870s into the early 1900s, this area was world-famous for its health spas and huge luxury resort hotels. Then, for various reasons, it fell into a state of disrepair and slowly lost its acclaim. Now it is a reasonably-priced, old-fashioned resort area.

The lake itself measures 25 miles by 8 miles. Spring-fed, it is the largest fresh-water lake totally in California (Lake Tahoe is partly in Nevada).

The scenic drive to get here takes you through the heart of the Wine Country, over rolling hills strewn with blazing wild flowers during the spring and with brilliantly-colored foliage during the fall. Try to make the drive during daylight; the one-lane road is tedious to drive at night, and you miss seeing the lovely scenery.

Clear Lake is situated on volcanic terrain, which gives it an unusual physical appearance and a profusion of hot springs. Many years ago the Pomo Indians lived here. They had a legend which said that if there is no snow on Mount Konocti in April, the volcano will erupt. If you believe in legends, be sure to check the April snowfall before you make your reservations.

■ *ROUTE*

Follow route to St. Helena and continue on Hwy 29. Located approximately 55 miles north of St. Helena.

■ *WHERE TO STAY*

Indian Beach Resort, *9945 E. Hwy 20 (P.O. Box 648), Glenhaven 95443, 707/998-3760; $22–$24; cribs, playground, beach, boat ramp, fishing pier, picnic and barbecue facilities, all cabins.*

Jules Resort, *14195 Lakeshore Dr. (P.O. Box 880), Clearlake Highlands 95422, 707/994-6491; $18–$20; cribs, TV, pool, sauna, playground, fishing pier, launching ramp, beach, game room, kitchens.*

Konocti Harbor Inn, *8727 Soda Bay Rd., Kelseyville 95451, 707/279-4281, toll-free reservations 800/862-4930; $34–$45, packages available (tennis, golf, fishing, fly-in); cribs, views, color TV, some kitchens, two-night minimum on weekends, laundromat, 8 tennis courts (fee), tennis lessons, 2 olympic-size swimming pools and 2 children's wading pools, playground, recreation area, running/bike trail, feature films; marina which rents equipment for fishing, waterskiing, and paddle boating; dining facilities (poolside snack bar, coffee shop, gourmet dining room); bar with live music in the evening.* That's quite a list of facilities. Believe it or not, there's more. College students are hired during the summer to entertain children ages 5–13, and the rates are reasonable. Babysitting can be arranged for younger children, and there is a special teen recreation center. Nestled in the shadow of Mount Konocti on the rim of the lake, the Konocti Harbor Inn enjoys a superb setting and is reminiscent of luxury resorts in Hawaii and a lot easier and less expensive to reach. Indeed, it is like a little city and is one of the most complete family resorts I've yet come across.

Konocti Princess, *daily in summer at 2pm; adults $5, children $3.*
   Take a cruise around the lake on this 100-passenger paddlewheel boat.

Pee Wee Golf, *daily in summer 10am–midnight; $1/18 holes.*

Lake-Vu Resort, *9505 Harbor Dr. (P.O. Box 12), Glenhaven 95443, 707/998-3331; $21.50; playground, pier, beach, all cabins with kitchens, two-night minimum on weekends.*

Redbud Lodge Resort, *3997 E. Hwy 20, Nice 95464, 707/274-1994; $23; beach, boat docks, pier, picnic area, barbecue facilities, play area, bait and tackle shop, paddle boat rentals, all cabins with kitchens.*

Trombetta's Beach Resort, *5865 Old Hwy 53 (P.O. Box 728), Clearlake Highlands 95422, 707/994-2417; $25; cribs, TV, boat rentals, boat ramp, pool, picnic area, playground, game room; RV hookups available.*

Will-O-Point Resort, *1 First St., Lakeport 95453, 707/263-5407; $31.80; cribs, TV, playground, recreation room, fishing pier, boat ramp, bait and tackle shop, laundromat, boat rentals, tennis court, sandy beach, dining facilities, cabins; campsites available.*

■ WHAT TO DO

Fishing, hunting, swimming, boating, rock hunting, golfing, and waterskiing (there are official races each month from April to September).

RUSSIAN RIVER

Russian River Chamber of Commerce
P.O. Box 331
(14034 Armstrong Woods Rd.)
Guerneville 95446
707/869-9009

- *A LITTLE BACKGROUND*
Once upon a time in the '20s and '30s, this was a summer
resort area for wealthy San Franciscans who traveled here
by ferry and train. Then it faded in popularity and became
a pleasant and uncrowded retreat. Today it is regaining its
former popularity in spite of its basic state of decay. A
large portion of the area's population used to be owners of
summer homes; they are gradually being replaced by younger,
permanent residents. Guerneville is the hub of the area and
is surrounded by many smaller towns.

- *ROUTE*
Located approximately 65 miles north of San Francisco.
Take Hwy 101 past Santa Rosa to Hwy 116 (River Road
West exit) to Guerneville.

- *STOPS ALONG THE WAY*
Korbel Champagne Cellars, *located just after you exit Hwy 101 onto*

97

River Road West, Guerneville, 707/887-2294; tours daily. If your kids are noisy and restless, skip the tour and head for the tasting room.

■ *WHERE TO STAY*

Brookside Lodge, *Hwy 116/Brookside Lane (P.O. Box 382), Guerneville, 707/869-2470; $35–$70; TV, pool, kitchens, recreation room, playground, evening programs in summer, some cottages.*

Hexagon House, *Guerneville Rd., Guerneville, 707/869-3991; $40–$60; cribs, two pools, TV, some sundecks, dining facilities, some cabins, two-night minimum on summer weekends.* This was once an art school studio.

Johnsons Lodge, *P.O. Box 386, Guerneville, 707/869-2022; $11–$20; open May–Sept only; TV, recreation area, beach on river.* Both hotel rooms and cabins are available; some are right on the river. Reservations are taken only for stays of at least a week, but there are often rooms available on a first-come, first-served basis. The beach is one of the best-equipped in the area. There is a slide in the water, picnic tables, and boat and beach paraphernalia for rent.

Northwood Lodge, *on Hwy 116 (P.O. Box 188), Monte Rio 95462, 707/865-2126; $34–$75; cribs, pool, whirlpool, river access, color TV.* This comfortable, modern motel is adjacent to a picturesque golf course. A few housekeeping cottages with fireplaces and bunkbeds are available.

Southside Resort, *13711 Hwy 16, Guerneville, 707/869-2690; $25–$26; private beach, nightly campfire, recreation area, kitchens, free movies.* Tucked under a bridge, these charming yellow cottages provide dots of color on the green, woodsy grounds. In July and August they are available only for a week at a time; you pay for six nights and get the seventh free. The beach here is shallow and safe for children. Camping facilities are also available.

■ *WHERE TO CAMP*

Austin Creek State Recreation Area, *17000 Armstrong Woods Rd., Guerneville, 707/869-2015; $3/night.* Located at the end of a narrow, steep, winding road three miles past Armstrong Redwoods State Reserve, the camping facilities here are "rustic." Nearby Armstrong Reserve has good hiking trails and in July and August often hosts free Sunday concerts in the outdoor Forest Theatre.

Duncans Mills Campground, *Hwy 116 (P.O. Box 57), Duncans Mills 95430, 707/865-2573; $6/tent, hookups available.* The restored and historic Duncans Mills railroad station now acts as the recep-

tion office for this riverside campground. Campsites are surrounded by natural shrubbery, and a private beach may be reached by a trail through the redwoods. The adjacent town, once a lumber village, has various shops as well as a restaurant, deli, and horse stables.

Southside Resort, *see page 98.*

■ *WHERE TO EAT*

The Lemonade Stand, *16208 1st St., Guerneville, 707/869-0721.* Sandwiches, hot dogs, and salads are available here as well as delicious freshly-made lemonade sweetened with honey.

The Occidental Three, *take Main St. through Monte Rio into Occidental.* All three of these restaurants serve multi-course, family-style Italian dinners. All have highchairs and booster seats and a reasonable plate charge for small children. All are medium priced and also offer ravioli and spaghetti dinners that are less expensive and include less side dishes. Reservations are highly recommended at prime dining times during the summer months. **Fiori's** (707/823-8188), **Negri's** (707/823-5301), **Union Hotel** (707/874-3662).

Rivers End Restaurant, *14 miles west of town, see page 66.*

Skippy's Hacienda Inn, *11190 McPeak Rd., Forestville, 707/887-2366; open three nights per week.* This is a comfortable family-style steak and seafood restaurant with bar. Call for the current hours.

The Village Inn, *River Blvd. (P.O. Box 56), Monte Rio, 707/865-1180; weekend brunch 10am–2pm.* This is where *Holiday Inn,* starring Bing Crosby, was filmed. Menu items are basically vegetarian with some fish and chicken entrees. Occasionally Tropical Pie, a great desert, is available. Prices are reasonable, and there is sometimes live music.

■ *WHAT TO DO*

Armstrong Redwoods State Reserve, *see* **Austin Creek State Recreation Area,** *page 98.*

Canoe Trips, *W. C. Bob Trowbridge, 20 Healdsburg Ave., Healdsburg 95448, 707/433-7247; March–Nov; $19/canoe.* The fee for these unguided trips includes life jackets, paddles, canoe transportation, and the ride back to your car. Children must be at least six, and reservations are necessary. You won't want to miss their bargain after-canoeing barbecue. Served at Healdsburg Memorial Beach from 4–7pm each weekend, the dinner includes a 10 oz. barbecued steak, barbecued chicken, French bread, salads, baked beans, and drinks. Children get a hamburger.

Cazadero, *west on Hwy 116.* Located on Austin Creek, this is a charming and tiny logging town.

Pee Wee Golf, *on Hwy 116; daily 11am–11pm.* **Abby's Playland** also has a super slide, ferris wheel, and moon walk. **J's Amusements** also has go-karts, tilt-a-whirl, scrambler, sock-a-tubes, and devil's coach. There is also a special room to check in toddlers while you have fun.

Swimming. Anywhere you choose to lay your blanket on the banks of the Russian River is bound to be nice. A choice spot is under the Monte Rio bridge. Parking and beach access are free. Another is Johnson's Beach. The beaches are rocky, so bring along waterproof sandals or tennis shoes to wear in the water.

SACRAMENTO

Sacramento Convention & Visitors Bureau
1100 14th St.
Sacramento 95814
916/449-5291

- ## GETTING THERE
  By Ferry. Delta Travel Agency, *1540 West Capitol Ave. (P.O. Box 813), West Sacramento 95691, 916/372-3690; $62/person, special rates for children.* Cruise through the Delta region to Sacramento. The package includes roundtrip boat tickets, bus transfers, and hotel accommodations in Sacramento. The boat departs from Pier 43½ in San Francisco.

  By Train. Amtrak trains leave for Sacramento daily from San Jose, San Francisco (with connections to Oakland), and Oakland. Special family fares are available. Call toll-free 800/648-3850 for fare and schedule information and to make reservations.

  Scenic Route by Car. Take Hwy 80 to Hwy 24 to Walnut Creek, Hwy 680 to Concord, Hwy 4 to Antioch, Hwy 160 to the outskirts of town, then Hwy 5 into Sacramento. Antioch has some restaurants (try the Riverview Lodge on H St.) and small shops near the river. It makes a good spot to stop for lunch. This route to Sacramento takes about six hours.

- ## SPECIAL EVENTS
  Dixieland Jubilee, *Memorial Day weekend, 1011 Second St., Sacramento 95814, 916/448-1251.*
  State Fair, *in August, 916/924-2000.*

■ STOPS ALONG THE WAY

The Nut Tree, *Hwy 80/Hwy 505, Vacaville, 707/448-1818; daily 7am–9pm; highchairs, children's portions; reservations suggested.* There is plenty to do at the Nut Tree besides eat. For a small fare a colorful miniature train transports passengers around the spacious grounds. Numerous shops are stocked with quality merchandise; the toy shop is a great place to shop for travel games and books for the kids. Outside there are free rocking horse rides, puppet shows, and climbing structures for the kids as well as a snack shop serving a memorable fresh orange slush and an assortment of other short-order items. The restaurant itself features striking architecture and a glass-enclosed area housing a variety of plants and exotic brightly-colored birds. The food is as tasty as the architecture is dramatic. An extensive choice of Gerber's baby food is featured on the menu as well as food for grownups. To top it all off, the personnel interact well with children—even messy, noisy ones!

■ WHERE TO STAY

Motel Row. Take a drive down the "Miracle Mile Motel Strip" located on West Capitol Ave.

■ WHERE TO EAT

Big Yellow House, *1788 Tribute Rd., 916/929-7573, 929-4610 for reservations & information; M–Th 5–9pm, F 5–10pm, Sat 4–10pm, Sun noon–9pm; highchairs, booster seats, special prices for children.* This is very similar to the Old Santa Cruz Railway (see page 23).

China Camp, *1015 The Embarcadero (in Old Sacramento), 916/441-7966; M–F 11:30am–2, 5:30–midnight, Sat 5:30–midnight, closed Sun; booster seats.* During the period after gold was discovered in Coloma in 1849, Chinese immigrants found it difficult to come by the ingredients and utensils traditionally used in their cooking. They learned to improvise by marinating their food with ethnic sauces. China Camp serves a re-creation of how that food most probably tasted. The rustic decor features brick walls, wooden booths, and architecture designed to give you the feeling you're inside an old mining camp. Unusual items include beef-in-clay-pot, the golden spike sandwich (pork with cucumber), and the gold miner's chicken salad (shredded chicken tossed with lettuce, rice noodles, sesame seeds, and nuts). As might be expected, there is an extensive selection of teas.

Fanny Ann's Saloon, *1023 Second St. (in Old Sacramento), 916/441-0505; daily from 11:30am.* The raucous ambience provides the makings for instant fun. Children and adults alike enjoy the casual atmosphere and inexpensive American-style fare which includes half-pound hamburgers, 9 inch hot dogs, and 12 oz. bowls of chili. When I inquired whether they had booster seats, the cheerful hostess answered, "I'll hold them on my lap."

Frank Fat's, *806 L St., 916/442-7092; M–F 11:30am–2pm, 4:30–midnight, Sat 5–midnight, Sun 4:30–10:30pm; highchairs, booster seats.* A Sacramento tradition since 1939, Frank Fat's is a favorite hangout for state politicians. The menu features Chinese food and good steaks.

Los Padres, *J St. (in Old Sacramento), 916/443-6376; M–F 11:30am–2pm, 5:30–10pm, Sat & Sun 11:30am–10pm; highchairs, booster seats, children's portions.* Located inside what was once the oldest furniture store in Sacramento, Los Padres is a quiet, nicely appointed restaurant featuring a portrayal of the California missions on its lovely old brick walls. The Early California/Mexican cuisine includes nachos (tortilla chips topped with refried beans and melted cheddar cheese), quesadillas (small corn tortillas topped with melted Jack cheese and guacamole), avocado soup, and a green enchilada (corn tortilla filled with king crab and guacamole and topped with green sauce and sour cream). Fresh, preservative-free tortillas are made in the restaurant's bakery located on the lower level. Food for take-out is also available there.

River Galley, *Levee Rd., Broderick, 916/372-0300; Tu–Sun 11am–2:30pm, 5–11pm, closed M; booster seats.* Specializing in seafood, this is Sacramento's only floating restaurant. Children may order half portions.

■ WHAT TO DO IN TOWN

California Almond Growers Exchange, *1802 C St., 916/442-0771; tours and movie M–F 10 am, 1, & 2pm.* Tour and taste at the world's largest almond factory, and see a movie about the history of almonds.

The Capitol, *building open daily 7am–9pm, public tours weekdays at 10:30am & 1:30pm, Senate & Assembly tours weekdays at 9:30, 10:30am, 1:30, & 2:30pm. Call 916/445-5200 for tour information.*

Capitol Park. Surrounding the Capitol, this 40-acre park consists of more than 400 varieties and species of trees and shrubs from around the world. Three self-guided tours are described in a free brochure available in room 134 of the Capitol building.

Crocker Art Museum, *216 O St., 916/446-4677; Tu 2–10pm, W–Sun 10am–5pm, closed M; 50¢.* The oldest art museum in the West, this gallery features special exhibitions in addition to its permanent collection. It is also the site for cultural events such as lectures, films, and Sunday afternoon concerts. Call for the current schedule.

Governor's Mansion, *16th/H Sts., 916/445-4209; daily 10am–5pm, tours every half hour 10am–4:30pm; adults 50¢, under 18 free (ticket is good all day in other state historical parks).* Built in 1878, this Victorian

Gothic structure was bought by the state in 1903 for $32,500! During the next 64 years it was home to 13 governors and their families. Now it is an interestingly-appointed museum.

Inner Tubing the American River. A good area is from Sailor Bar to Watt Avenue Bridge.

Music Circus, *15th/G Sts. adjacent to the Sacramento Civic Theater, 916/441-3163; $8.50–$11.50.* Claiming to be "the only tent theater west of the Mississippi" and seating 2,500, the Music Circus presents summer stock musicals which are suitable for the entire family. Call for the current schedule.

Old Sacramento. Old Sacramento is said to be the largest historic preservation project in the West. The old buildings, wooden sidewalks, and brick streets make it a 28-acre living museum of the Old West. Restaurants and shops as well as historic exhibits make it an entertaining and educational spot to visit. Motorized cable cars will transport you to the downtown shopping mall, allowing for a scenic way to rest for a few minutes after strolling through this extensive area.

WHAT TO SEE:

The California State Railroad Museum, *Front St.; daily 10am–5pm; adults 50¢, under 18 free.* Inside a reconstructed train depot, visitors step back in time to the days when riding the train was the chic way to go. When you pay your admission at the old-fashioned ticket window, you will be given a "tour wand" which will enable you to hear prerecorded descriptions of the various displays which include three steam locomotives from the 1870s (see photo opposite), two wooden passenger cars from the 1880s and '90s, a private car decorated in Victorian style, and some freight cars. Children will be ecstatic to learn that they are given their very own wand to hold.

The Eagle Theater, *925 Front St., 916/446-6761; Tu–Sun 10am–5pm, closed M; performances Th–Sun evenings, 8:30pm curtain; $3.50–$4.50; reservations suggested.* A reconstruction of the first theater on the West Coast, the Eagle now features regular melodrama performances by local actors. It also hosts occasional special events. Call for current schedule.

SNACK STOPS:

Mrs. Churchill's Cookie Company, *1102 2nd St.* On a hot day you can experience an old-fashioned pleasure by stopping here for homemade cookies and fresh-squeezed lemonade.

The Sacramento Sweets Co., *906 2nd St.* Munch on samples while you try to decide which of the tempting sweets to buy. My kids were suckers for the delicious caramel apples.

State Indian Museum, *2618 K St.; daily 10am–5pm; free.* Located adjacent to Sutter's Fort, the Indian Museum was established in 1940 and features continuously changing exhibits of Indian life. A permanent basket collection and samples of bark clothing are

particularly interesting.

Sutter's Fort State Historic Park, *2701 L St.; daily 10am–5pm; adults 50¢, under 18 free.* A reconstruction of the settlement founded in 1839 by Captain John A. Sutter, this fort has been restored to appear as it did in 1848. Exhibits include carpenter, cooper, and blacksmith shops as well as prison and living quarters. Electronic headsets are given to visitors when they pay their admission; they allow for a two-hour, self-guided tour of the site.

Swimming in the American River, *take Watt exit off Hwy 50 near Carmichael.* Here you can swim in the river or sun on the sandy banks.

W. G. Stone Lock, *on Jefferson Blvd. at entrance to Port of Sacramento, 916/371-7540; daily dawn–dusk; free.* From an overlook, visitors may view this 600 foot long lock in action. Its schedule of operation depends on ship traffic.

William Land Park. This 236-acre park is bounded by Sutterville Rd., 13th Ave., Freeport Blvd., and Riverside Blvd.

    Zoo, *daily 9am–5pm; adults $1.50, 6–12 75¢, 5 and under free.*

Fairytale Town, *open Tu–Sun 10am–5pm, closed M; adults 75¢, 3–12 25¢.* Nursery rhymes and fairy tales come alive in this amusement park.

- # *WHAT TO DO NEARBY*

Princeton Ferry, *9 miles east of Hwy 5 on Norman Rd. in Princeton south of Chico; daily 6am–midnight; free.* A leftover from the Gold Rush days, this is the last ferry on the Sacramento river. Used mainly by farmers to reach their orchards and rice paddies, this cable-operated ferry takes only two minutes to cross the river. Current plans are to eventually replace the ferry with a new-fangled bridge.

NATIONAL PARKS

YOSEMITE NATIONAL PARK

National Park Service
P.O. Box 577
Yosemite National Park 95389
209/372-4611

- *GETTING THERE*
  If you want to take a bus, contact California Parlor Car Tours
  (Jack Tar Hotel, Van Ness/Geary, San Francisco 94101, 415/
  495-1444) for information. Rates for two nights lodging and
  meals are $154/adult, $133/children, under 6 free.

- *SPECIAL EVENTS*
  Spending Christmas at the Ahwahnee Hotel and enjoying the
  memorable Bracebridge Dinner is a pleasure not many will get
  to enjoy. This expensive experience ($60/person) requires that
  participants make their reservations a full year in advance.
  Since 1927 the fare at the elegant dinner, held on the evenings
  of December 24 and 25, has been traditional foods such as
  Peacock Pie, Boar's Head, and Wassail. Pageantry, readings,
  and carols entertain between courses.

■ *A LITTLE BACKGROUND*

A $3 admission fee is collected at all park entrances. Visitors are given a free activities newsletter, *The Yosemite Guide,* and a park map.

Among the scenic wonders here are El Capitan, the largest piece of exposed granite in the world, and Yosemite Falls, the highest in the northern hemisphere. Remember that the falls and rivers can be dangerous as well as beautiful; keep a good grip on your children when hiking.

> "Yosemite Park is a place of rest. A refuge . . . in which one gains the advantage of both solitude and society . . . none can escape its charms. Its natural beauty cleanses and warms like fire, and you will be willing to stay forever. . . ."
>
> *—John Muir*

■ *ROUTE*

Located approximately 200 miles east of San Francisco. Take Hwy 80 to Hwy 580 to Hwy 205 to Hwy 120.

■ *STOPS ALONG THE WAY*

You will be passing lots of fruit and nut stands, and there are many cafes in the little towns on Hwy 120.

Hershey Chocolate Factory and Confectionery Plant, *1400 S. Yosemite Rd., Oakdale 95361, 209/847-0381; M–F 8:15am–3pm, closed weekends; free.* Tours here last 30 minutes and, at the end, all visitors are given a chocolate bar. More are for sale at the Visitor's Center.

Pollardville Ghost Town, *10464 N. Hwy 99, three miles north of Stockton, 209/931-0272, 931-4571; weekends noon–5:30pm; adults $1.50, children 75¢.* This reconstructed ghost town features a narrow-gauge railroad (50¢/ride) and staged gunfights.

Riverbank and Stanislaus County Cheese Companies *(from Modesto take Hwy 108 to Riverbank);* **Stanco,** *3141 Sierra Ave., 209/869-2558, daily 8am–6pm, tours daily;* **Riverbank,** *6603 Second St., 209/ 869-2803, daily 8am–6pm, tours weekdays 8, 9, & 10am.* Specialty cheeses are cheddars, jack and teleme. Picnic supplies may be purchased in their delicatessens.

Oakwood Lake Resort, *874 E. Woodward, Manteca 95336, 209/239-9566; day use: adults $2, 5–11 $1; camping: $7.50–$9.50/night.* Water activities are the main form of entertainment here. Small children will enjoy the shallow swimming lagoon and two large

playground areas—one of which is right in the water. A deeper area is available for swimmers, plus paddle boats ($3), jet skis ($5), and bumper boats ($1.25). But the main attraction is the eight fiberglass waterslides, each with over 60 feet of underground tunnel and two 360° turns. Riders are charged $2.50/half hour of continuous sliding. Children measuring less than 42 inches tall must ride with an adult. One slide is set aside for small children and the timid. There is no charge for using it. Bring tennis shoes or water sandals to protect feet from scrapes.

■ *CHILDCARE*

Make arrangements through a clerk at any of the hotel desks. Sitters are recruited from the employee residence halls.

Supervised care for children over 3 is available at the Ski Tots Club at Badger Pass in winter and in Curry Village in summer.

In the summer a Junior Ranger program is available for children. It is broken into sections for grades 3–6 and grades 7 and up.

■ *WHERE TO STAY*

Yosemite is always crowded, especially in the summer, and reservations are essential. Call 209/373-4171 for information or to make reservations at any of the park facilities. Rates range from $10.50 to $60. Ask about the special "Midweek Winter Package."

Ahwahnee Hotel; *pool, playground, tennis courts, climbing facilities.* This is a very sedate luxury hotel.

Curry Village. Accommodations and facilities are similar to Yosemite Lodge (see below), but tent cabins are also available.

Tuolumne Meadows Lodge; *dining facilities, all tent cabins.* This facility is located at the eastern entrance (Tioga Pass).

Wawona Hotel, *located at the south entrance (Hwy 41), near the Mariposa Grove of Big Trees, 30 miles from the valley; pool, tennis court, 9-hole golf course, dining facilities; closed in winter.* Built in 1856, this Victorian hotel is less crowded than valley accommodations and features 66 rooms furnished with antiques.

White Wolf Lodge. Located at Tioga Pass, 31 miles from the valley.

Yosemite Lodge; *cribs, pool, bike rentals, dining facilities.* Accommodations vary from frugal (*old* cabins without water) to luxurious (modern hotel rooms).

■ *WHERE TO CAMP*

Campgrounds are open April–October. Make reservations through Ticketron. See page 192.

■ *WHERE TO EAT*

Ahwahnee Hotel, *209/372-4611 x408; daily 7:30–9:30am, noon–1:30pm, 6:30–8:30pm; highchairs, booster seats, children's portions; reservations essential.* The best time to dine in the rustic splendor of this elegant dining room is during daylight hours. Only then can you take full advantage of the spectacular views of the valley offered by the 50 foot high floor-to-ceiling windows. At dinner men are expected to wear a coat and tie and women to dress accordingly. Guests of the hotel receive the select dining times, so be prepared for either an early or late seating. Children fit in best at breakfast or lunch; for dinner, arrange for a babysitter.

Curry Village Cafeteria; *all meals.* It is efficient and inexpensive.

Four Seasons Restaurant, *Yosemite Lodge; all meals; highchairs, booster seats.* The dinner menu here offers good old American fare—steak, fried chicken, fish, and hamburgers.

Mountain Room Bar, *Yosemite Lodge.* This is a great place to get rid of the kinks you develop during your long drive in. While you relax and await your dinner reservation, you can rub elbows with the local rock climbers who hang out here.

Mountain Room Broiler, *Yosemite Lodge; open for dinner only; highchairs, booster seats.* Stunning floor-to-ceiling windows allow you to observe Yosemite Falls while you dine on steak, trout, lobster, corn-on-the-cob, artichokes, and delicious hot cheese bread. The walls are papered in striking black and white photo murals.

■ *WHAT TO DO*

Bicycling, *rentals available at Yosemite Lodge (x208, 9am–5pm daily) and Curry Village (x200, 8am–8pm daily) April–Oct; $1.50/hour, child carriers available.* A bicycling map and information about ranger-guided bike tours may be obtained when you rent your bike. Each spring and fall there is a Yosemite Bike Rally. For information write Yosemite Bike Rally, c/o Yosemite Park or call 209/372-4611 x208.

Bus Tours, *209/372-4611 x240.*

Check the *Yosemite Guide* for complete information. Whether you drive or take the guided tour, don't miss the **Mariposa Grove of Big Trees.** Several hundred giant sequoias are located in this 250-acre grove. From May to October free open air trams take visitors

on a guided tour. In winter, this is a great spot for cross-country skiing.

You can also visit the **Pioneer History Center** (daily in summer 9am–5pm; weekends in fall; rides 75¢) where you will see demonstrations of soap making, yarn spinning, rail splitting, and other pioneer crafts and get a chance to ride on a stagecoach. Sometimes there is even an old-fashioned square dance.

Glacier Point, *an hour drive from the valley.* From this spot you can enjoy a 270° panorama of the high country, or you can look down 3,242 feet for a bird's-eye view of the valley. Several trails lead from here down to the valley. Consider arriving here in the morning and then spending the afternoon hiking back down.

Hiking. Enjoy a ranger-guided walk or take any of the numerous self-guided trails. Check in the park brochure for maps. Each day a two-hour camera walk is led by a skilled photographer.

Indian Cultural Museum, *located next to the Yosemite Village Visitor Center; W–Sun 9am–noon, 1–4pm.* Artifacts, cultural demonstrations, and recorded chants of the Awanichi Indians may be enjoyed at this museum. Behind the museum is a self-guided trail which points out the plants the Indians used in making their food, clothing, and shelters. It also passes through a reconstructed Indian village.

Inner Tube Float Trip. Scenic and calm is the area on the Merced River between Pines Campground and El Capitan Bridge.

Movies. Scenic movies are shown nightly. Check the *Yosemite Guide* for times and locations.

Ranger Talks. Consult the *Yosemite Guide* for times and locations.

Rock Climbing Lessons, *Village Sport Shop and Tuolumne Meadows, 209/372-4611 x244 and 209/372-4505 (summer only).* Learn rock climbing at Yosemite Mountaineering School, one of the finest schools in the world. Basic classes ($16/person) are held daily. A two-hour non-participation class is held each day at 10am and 1pm. Participants see a film and then an actual demonstration.

Valley Stables *(other locations) guided two-hour horse trips leave at 8am, 10am, and 1pm, $8.50/person; half-day mule trips/$10, all-day $16.* Believed to have the largest rental stock in the United States, these stables can also arrange for custom pack and/or fishing trips. Burros may be rented by parents for their children to ride; parents must lead the burros. Inquire about the special "burro picnic" for kids.

Yosemite Mountain Sugar Pine Railroad, *on Hwy 41 four miles from the valley, Fish Camp, 209/683-7273; daily in summer 10am–4pm; weekends and holidays Sept. & May, closed Nov–April; adults $4, 3–12 $2, under 3 free.* Take a four-mile trip on this narrow-gauge steam railway. You may stop off midway for a picnic and hike. In the winter inner tubes are available for rental. There are sometimes moonlight rides on summer Saturday nights.

Winter Activities, *see pages 188, 189 and 190.*

SEQUOIA AND KINGS CANYON NATIONAL PARKS

Hospitality Service
Sequoia National Park 93262
Sequoia, 209/565-3373
Kings Canyon, 209/335-2314

■ *A LITTLE BACKGROUND*

Though they are located just south of Yosemite National Park, these two scenic National Parks are often overlooked by travelers. It's a shame because they, too, offer spectacular scenery

and are much less crowded. Their main attraction is the enor-
mous Sequoia trees located in the Giant Forest. The largest
tree is the General Sherman Tree—a towering 275 feet high,
36½ feet in diameter, and 3 to 4,000 years old—higher than
Niagara Falls, as wide as a city street, and already middle-aged
when Christ was born! It is said to be the largest living thing
on this planet. Admission to the parks is $2/car per day.

- *ROUTE*
Located approximately 250 miles southeast of San Francisco.
Take Hwy 80 to Hwy 580 to Hwy 99 south to Hwy 180 east.

- *WHERE TO STAY*

Park Lodging, *209/565-3373; $14–$33; cribs, dining facilities, some kitchens.* At Sequoia lodging varies from spartan to deluxe cabins.
Kings Canyon has similar facilities but in general they are less luxurious. Arrangements can be made to backpack into a camp facility
with furnished tents. Campsites are available on a first-come, first-

served basis. The best way to make reservations is to send for the park brochure which explains the various options in detail. If interested, ask about the special ski packages.

If for some reason you are unable to get lodging at the park facilities, there are two privately-owned lodges in Wilsonia:

Kings Canyon Lodge, *P.O. Box 853, Kings Canyon 93633, 209/335-2311.*

Wilsonia Lodge, *P.O. Box 808, Kings Canyon 93633, 209/335-2310.*

Also see **Montecito Sequoia Lodge,** page 172.

■ *WHAT TO DO*

Bicycle Rentals, *in Cedar Grove.*

Crystal Cave; *daily in summer 9:30am–3pm; 50¢.* This cave is reached by walking a ½ mile trail.

Grant Grove Visitor Center, *daily in summer 8am–8pm, rest of year 9am–5pm; free.* See exhibits on the area's wildlife as well as displays on the Indians and sequoias. Taped guides are available for rent. Inquire here about the schedule of **nature walks** and **evening campfire programs.**

Fishing. Good spots abound.

Horse Rentals, *in Cedar Grove, Giant Forest at Wolverton, General Grant Grove, and Owens Valley.*

Self-guided Trails. Over 900 miles of trails are in these parks.

Swimming and Sunbathing, *at "Bikini Beach."*

Unusual Trees. Most of these will be encountered as you drive along the 46-mile General's Highway which connects the two parks.

    Auto Log. You can drive your car onto it to take a photograph.

    Room Tree. Climb a ladder and enter down through a burn hole into the "room" and then exit through another burn hole.

    Senate Group and House Group of Sequoias. These are the most symmetrically formed and nearly perfect of the sequoias.

    Tunnel Log. You can drive your car inside this tunnel carved through a tree which fell across the road long ago.

Winter Activities. See **Sequoia Ski Touring** page 189, **Montecito Sequoia Nordic Ski Center** page 188, **snow play** page 189.

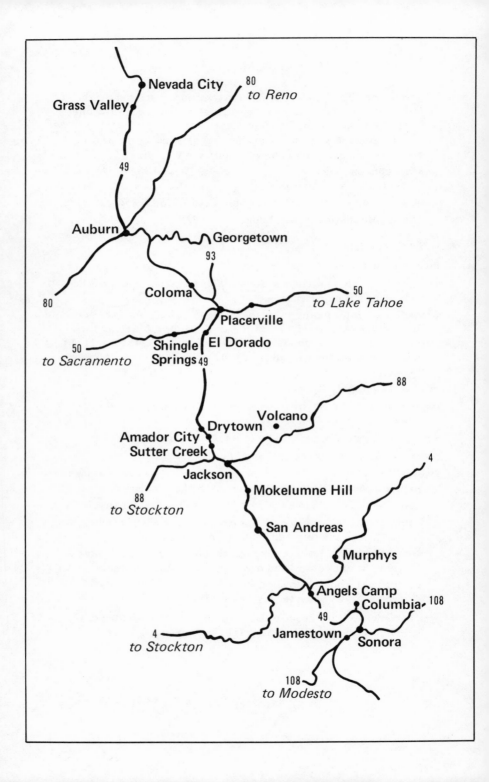

GOLD RUSH COUNTRY

■ *A LITTLE BACKGROUND*
Technically the Mother Lode stretches from Melones to
Auburn, where the primary gold vein was located. It takes at
least three or four days to see the entire area. If you are going for only a weekend, don't attempt to drive the entire
route from south to north. Visit just one portion, and then
go back another time to see the rest. Take the time to explore side roads off Hwy 49 and visit towns whose names in-
trigue you. Bear in mind that many of the interesting hotels
in this area are European-style with bathrooms down the hall.

Because the area is steeped in history, I recommend a jaunt
to the library for some background information. Two books
about the area which you might enjoy reading out loud with
your trip companions are *The Celebrated Jumping Frog of
Calaveras County* by Samuel L. Clemens (Mark Twain) and
The Luck of Roaring Camp by Bret Harte. Here's some advice
on staking a claim:

> "A gold mine is a hole in the ground with a liar at the
> entrance."
>
> *—Mark Twain*

■ *ROUTE*

Located approximately 140 miles east of San Francisco. Take Hwy 80 to Hwy 580 to Hwy 205 to Hwy 120 to Hwy 49. A good map of the Gold Rush area is available free from the Auburn Chamber of Commerce. See page 143.

JAMESTOWN

■ *WHERE TO STAY*

Jamestown Hotel, *P.O. Box 539, 95327, 209/984-3902; $40–$58; cribs, continental breakfast included, dining facilities.* Built in the 1850s and recently remodeled, the Jamestown Hotel is furnished with Victorian antiques and cozied up with patchwork quilts. Caged birds sing in the halls. Many rooms are suites complete with sitting room; all have private baths. Breakfast is served in your room or outside on the deck.

Railtown 1897, *see next page.*

■ *WHERE TO EAT*

Gold Country Ice Cream Parlor, *18231 Main St., 209/984-8961; F–Sun 10am–9pm, Tu–Th 10am–5pm, closed M.* Known for its double banana split, this ice cream parlor actually maintains a list of all those who have eaten one and how long it took them.

Mountain Steamer Pizza, *Main St., 209/984-3722; M–Th 11am–10pm, F & Sat 11am–11pm, Sun 4–10pm.* Specialties here are pizza, steamed clams, submarine sandwiches, and pasties.

Railtown 1897, *see below.*

The Smoke, *Main St., 209/984-3733; W–M noon–10pm, closed Tu.* Inexpensive and friendly, this restaurant serves tasty Chinese and Mexican cuisine.

■ *WHAT TO DO*

Railtown 1897, *on Fifth Ave. in Jamestown (Sierra Railroad Company, 2143 Mono Way, Sonora 95370), 209/984-3953.* The popular dining excursions have been discontinued, but you can still dine in the stationary Silver Plate Dining Car. Afterwards enjoy the Roundhouse tour, a walking tour with stops at the blacksmith shop, machine shop, turntable, and the six-stall roundhouse where the steam locomotives and antique railroad cars are maintained and restored (daily in summer 9am–5pm, weekends rest of year; adults $1.55, 5–15 70¢, under 5 free). Refurbished pullman cars may be reserved for overnight accommodations.

SONORA

Tuolumne County Chamber of Commerce
P.O. Box 277
Sonora 95370
209/532-4212

Sonora Pass Vacationland
P.O. Box 607
Columbia 95310

■ *A LITTLE BACKGROUND*

Located near Jamestown, the bustling Gold Rush town of Sonora is a popular layover spot for skiers and travelers on their way to summer cabins and recreation. Because it is a crossroads, the town has been built up a bit more than most Gold Rush towns, and it is far from quiet. But if you get off the main streets, you'll find a taste of the old Sonora—Victorian homes, quiet streets, and a little bit of a country feeling.

■ *WHERE TO STAY*

Gunn House, *286 S. Washington St,, 209/532-3421; $26.50-$31.80; cribs, pool, TV.* Once the residence of Dr. Lewis C. Gunn, this two-story house is currently serving as a motel. Beautifully restored and decorated, the antique-filled rooms are a delight to stay in.

Sonora Towne House Motel, *350 S. Washington St., 209/532-3633; $26-$30; pool, color TV.* Located in downtown Sonora, the Towne House provides modern accommodations.

■ *WHERE TO EAT*

Europa Coffee Shop, *275 S. Washington St., 209/532-9957; open daily 24 hours; highchairs, booster seats.* Popular with local residents, the Europa serves a choice of over 45 dinner entrees and is well-known for its homemade pies. Everything is made from scratch. The only problem you're likely to have here is deciding what to order.

Hong Kong Restaurant, *267 S. Washington St., 209/532-1544; W-M 11am-9:30pm, closed Tu; highchairs, booster seats.* This comfortable restaurant specializes in Cantonese Chinese as well as American fare.

Howard's, *35 N. Washington St., 209/532-1576; Tu-Sat 5-10pm, Sun 4-9pm, closed M; highchairs, booster seats, children's portions; reservations suggested.* The atmosphere in the huge dining room at Howard's, built in the 1870s, is noisy. The waitresses are very helpful and accustomed to dealing with children. The homemade dinners include soup, salad, vermicelli, vegetable, baked or whipped potatoes, toasted French bread, dessert, and coffee or tea. Adult entrees include steak, prime rib, lobster tail, pot roast, pan-fried chicken, halibut, chicken-fried steak, and more! Children choose from fried chicken, filet of sole, and ground round. To top it all off, the prices are quite reasonable. Arrive at Howard's hungry.

The Miner's Shack, *157 S. Washington, 209/532-5252; M-F 6am-6pm, Sat 8am-6pm, closed Sun.* Said to be a goldminer who discovered he made more money at cooking for other miners than at mining, owner Joshua gives diners a choice of 32 omelettes, numerous sandwiches, and assorted chicken items.

Yerby's Deli, *229 S. Washington St., 209/532-4472; daily 7:30am-8pm, F & Sat until 9pm, Sun until 5:30pm.* A great spot to pick up picnic supplies, Yerby's has barbecue chicken and ribs as well as other hot and cold deli items.

■ *WHAT TO DO IN TOWN*

Sonora County Museum, *158 W. Bradford Ave., 209/532-4212; M-F*

9am–noon, 1–5pm, also on weekends in summer 10am–3pm; free.
Located inside a jail built in 1866, this museum boasts a $40,000
gold collection and various relics from the Gold Rush era.

■ WHAT TO DO NEARBY

Westside & Cherry Valley Railway, *(P.O. Box 1017), eight miles from
town, Tuolumne 95379, 209/928-4282; daily in summer 10am–
10pm, weekends rest of year 10am–8pm; ticket books: adults $6,
children $4, under 3 free.* Enjoy a day in the country as it would
have occurred in the early 1900s. Take a trip on the authentic
logging railroad, a spin in one of the antique firetrucks or busses,
or a cruise on a sternwheel steam barge. A Mewuk Indian village
offers a chance to learn more about the customs and beliefs of
this Indian group. And if you're around at dinner time, you might
enjoy a dinner cruise featuring a choice of Mexican or American
cuisine.

COLUMBIA STATE HISTORICAL PARK

P.O. Box 151
Columbia 95310
209/532-4301

■ *SPECIAL EVENTS*
Fire Muster, *May.* Contact above address for details. For description of a muster, see page 53.

■ *A LITTLE BACKGROUND*
Referred to as the "Gem of the Southern Mines," Columbia in its heyday had a population of 15,000 and produced $87 million in gold. Since 1945 Columbia has been a reconstructed Gold Rush town. It keeps getting better all the time. Open daily from 9am to 5pm, this State Historical Park allows no automobiles on its streets. Among the authentic shops and businesses in town are a grocery store, blacksmith shop, harness and saddlery shop, firehouse, dry goods store, barbershop, gold mine tour, confectionery, portrait studio, candy store, antique shop, and newspaper office. There are also plenty of picnic spots, entertainment, and dining facilities.

■ *WHERE TO STAY*
City Hotel, *on Main St. (P.O. Box 1870), 209/532-1479; $33.50–$42.50; cribs, includes continental breakfast, dining facilities.* State and federal agencies have provided almost three-quarters of a million dollars to reconstruct this hotel just as it was when it was originally built in 1856. Rooms are furnished with authentic Victorian antiques from the collection of the California State Parks Department. The staff is augmented by cheerful, eager-to-please students from the Columbia Junior College Hospitality Management program. Decked out in costumes appropriate to times past, they fluff up your pillows and tend to your needs. All guests are given use of a wicker basket packed with bathing necessities—including a shower cap, slippers, and robe! Guests are encouraged to congregate in the parlor and entertain themselves with conversation and games. To say the very least, the City Hotel is an experience.
Columbia Gem Motel, *Hwy 49 (P.O. Box 874), 209/532-4508; $27–$35; cribs.* Typical motel rooms greet guests inside the tiny cottages scattered in an attractive pinetree setting.

■ WHERE TO CAMP

Yankee Hill Campground, *located 3/10 mile beyond the Post Office on Yankee Hill Rd. (P.O. Box 850), 209/532-9539; $9.50-$11/night.* Built on the site of an old marble quarry, this campground features a playground and pool as well as numerous hiking trails.

■ WHERE TO EAT

Candy Kitchen, *Main St.* The Nelson family makes homemade candies from recipes over 100 years old. They've been doing it for over 30 years. Made from natural ingredients, often with antique utensils, these candies are hard to pass by without sampling.

City Hotel Dining Room, *Main St., 209/532-1479; W-Sun 11:30am-2pm, Tu-Sun 5:30-9pm; highchairs, booster seats.* Serving elegant continental cuisine (artichoke hearts stuffed with spinach, roast duck with orange sauce, marinated hare in game sauce, roast quail), this restaurant is beautifully appointed with lovely china and glassware. A former chef at Ernie's in San Francisco runs what has been called the most expensive kitchen in the state. You'll want your children dressed in their finest and displaying their best manners when you bring them here. The **What Cheer Saloon** (daily 4:30-11pm) adjoins.

Columbia House, *Main St.; daily for breakfast and lunch, in summer also dinner; highchairs, booster seats.* This casual, cafeteria-style restaurant serves inexpensive meals. Noteworthy are the sourdough pancakes, homemade berry pie, and bean pot.

Firemen's Retreat, *Broadway/State (P.O. Box 588), 209/532-6613; open daily.* This old-fashioned ice cream parlor dispenses sodas, sundaes, and shakes as well as regular and baby-size cones.

J. B. Douglass Saloon, *Main St.; daily 10am-5pm.* Listen to the honky-tonk sound of a player piano while you sit at the bar or at tables munching on a sandwich (or maybe a hot pretzel topped with melted cheese) and sipping a scuttle of sarsaparilla.

■ WHAT TO DO

A. De Cosmos Daguerrean Studio, *State St. (P.O. Box 550).* Dress up in old-fashioned costumes provided by the studio and have a family portrait taken. Get here early to take a reservation number; the wait is sometimes quite long. Prices vary with photo size and number of people. This makes a spectacular souvenir.

Fallon House Theatre, *209/532-4644; performances during summer only, Tu-Sat 8:30pm curtain, 2pm matinees on weekends, dark M; adults $3-$5, under 12 $1.50-$4; reservations essential.* This theatre has been in operation since the 1880s. Now plays are performed by the

University of the Pacific repertory theatre company. Write or call for current information and schedule.

Fandango Hall Theatre, *Main St., 209/532-7041; performance schedule irregular, call for current details.* After buying tickets hawked on the street by a comely lass, you will descend into the mysterious, noisy cellar or "palace of pleasure." Audiences are treated to live performances of such melodrama classics as *The Drunkard.* A honky-tonk piano helps things along, and the audience is encouraged to hiss the villain and cheer the hero.

Hidden Treasure Gold Mine, *P.O. Box 712, 209/532-9693; tours daily 9:30am–4pm except Oct–May when they are closed on M; adults $4, 5–16 $2.75, under 5 free, special family rates.* Discovered in 1879, this gold mine is still active. The guided tour leaves by bus from the Columbia Mine Supply Store and then walks through 700 feet of tunnel. A working milling operation may also be viewed. For an additional charge of $4/person, a gold strike is guaranteed in a nearby panning area.

Stagecoach Ride, *P.O. Box 681, 209/532-1035; $1.50/person, under 3 free if sitting on a lap.* In the summer a surrey with a fringe on top takes riders on evening tours of the town (adults $1.50, 6–12 $1, under 6 free).

■ WHAT TO DO NEARBY

Nature Walk, *Columbia Junior College (take Parrott's Ferry Rd. exit off Hwy 49, turn right onto Sawmill Flat Rd. and go 1½ miles to the*

campus entrance). The nature trail begins near the Natural Resources
building. A free brochure, which explains characteristic geologic for-
mations and lists the plants you will see, is available at the trailhead.

Picnic. Take Italian Bar Rd. until it turns into a dirt road. Continue on
a few miles into the Stanislaus Forest to find a pleasant picnic spot
by the river.

Yosemite Airlines, *at Pine Mountain Lake Airport (P.O. Box 330), 209/
532-6946, call collect for reservations.* Take a scenic airtour of the
Yosemite or Gold Rush area. Flights and packages are available from
Oakland and San Francisco to Columbia.

MURPHYS

■ *A LITTLE BACKGROUND*

A map to the town's buildings and sights is available from
many town merchants and at the check-in desk in the hotel.
Murphys is sometimes referred to as the "Queen of the Sierra."

■ *WHERE TO STAY*

Murphys Hotel, *P.O. Box 329, 95247, 209/728-3454 (call for reservations daily 9am–4pm); $29; dining facilities.* Now a National Histori-
cal Monument, the rooms located in this old hotel are said to have
provided overnight lodging for such Gold Rush era luminaries as U. S.
Grant, J. P. Morgan, Mark Twain, Horatio Alger, John Muir, and
Black Bart. There are also modern motel rooms, with no legends
attached, available adjacent to the hotel. I have stayed in both and
find the hotel rooms to be immeasurably more interesting but with
one big drawback. The noisy hotel bar, reputed to be the best in the
Mother Lode, is kept jumping until the wee hours by townspeople
and travelers alike. If you want to sleep, opt for the motel rooms.
In the winter, ask about the special skier rates.

■ *WHERE TO EAT*

Murphys Restaurant, *in the hotel; daily for all three meals; highchairs,
booster seats, children's portions.* This noisy, cheerful dining spot is
decorated with red-checked tablecloths and staffed with pleasant
waitresses. The huge meals are standard, hearty American fare. One
morning at breakfast, my family was seated at a huge round table
which, due to crowded conditions, we were asked to share with some
local residents. The resulting conversation was most enjoyable, and
we left richer, having been exposed to an insider's view of the area.

Peppermint Stick, *across the street from the hotel, 209/728-3570; Tu–Sun 10:30am–5pm, closed M.* Stop inside for an old-fashioned soda or homemade candy treat.

■ *WHAT TO DO IN TOWN*

Black Bart Players, *P.O. Box 104, 209/728-3379; weekend performances in April & Nov; $3.50/person.* Call or write for the schedule of melodrama performances.

Old Timers Museum, *across the street from the hotel; in summer W–Sun 10am–5pm, weekends only rest of year.* Visit the oldest stone building in town, circa 1856, to view interesting memorabilia from the past.

Mercer Caverns, *one mile north of town off Hwy 4 (P.O. Box 509), 209/728-2101; daily in summer 9am–5pm, weekends rest of year 11am–4pm; adults $2.75, 5–11 $1.25, under 5 free.* Thirty-minute guided tours leave regularly to go through this well-lighted 55° cavern.

■ *WHAT TO DO NEARBY*

Calaveras Big Trees State Park, *15 miles east of town (P.O. Box 120), Arnold 95223, 209/795-2334; daily; $2/car.* If you visit in the winter while there is still snow on the ground, be sure to inquire about the ranger-led snowshoe and cross-country ski tours (see also page 188). The Big Trees nature trail, leading through groves of giant redwoods, is enjoyable any time. This ancient forest houses the mammoth and now rare sequoia variety of redwood. A trail guide to the

quiet, scenic walk is available at the trailhead. Other trails are in the park along with picnic and barbecue facilities and campgrounds. In warm weather the Beaver Creek Picnic Area has a wading and swimming area appropriate for children. For a snack or to pick up picnic provisions, stop in Arnold where there are several delis, markets, and restaurants.

Moaning Cave, *5150 Moaning Cave Rd. (P.O. Box 78), Vallecito 95251, 209/736-2708; daily in summer 9am–6pm, weekends rest of year 10am–5pm; adults $3, under 11 $1.50, babies free.* Claiming to be California's deepest public cavern, Moaning Cave features a descent down a 100 foot spiral staircase. A pleasant picnic area is available outside.

ANGELS CAMP

- ## SPECIAL EVENTS

The third weekend in May features the annual **Calaveras County Jumping Frog Jubilee** a la Mark Twain. Champion frogs have recorded jumps of over 20 feet and have earned as much as $1,200. The area is mobbed for this event. If you're still interested, contact the Calaveras Fairgrounds Office, P.O. Box 96, Angels Camp 95222, 209/736-2561 for current information. Gate admission is $4–$5.50/adults, $2–$3.50/children.

- ## WHERE TO EAT

Emporium Ice Creme Parlour,
1262 S. Main St., 209/736-2676; daily 10:30am–10pm; children's portions. Located inside an old bank filled with many other shops, this ice cream parlor dispenses sarsaparilla, ice cream sundaes, sandwiches, and hot dogs. Diners exit through the 7,000 lb. vault door into an adjacent bookstore.

Picnic. There are informal picnic areas by the river and in **City Park,** where there are picnic tables and a play area as well. You might want to stop at **Angels Bakery** (1277 Main St., 209/736-4360; M–Sat 7:30am–5:30pm, closed Sun) to pick up some cheese & salt breadsticks, garlic bread, or fruit bars and at the **Bazinett Coffee Shop** (1276 Main St.; daily 6am–9pm) for some chicken & fries to go.

■ *WHAT TO DO*

Angels Camp Museum, *753 Main St., 209/736-2963; daily in summer 9am–4:30pm, in winter 11am–4pm and closed Tu & W; adults 50¢, 6-12 25¢.* Notable here is the assemblage of wagons and buggies and an extensive rock collection.

SAN ANDREAS

Calaveras County Chamber of Commerce
P.O. Box 177
(30 S. Main)
San Andreas 95249
209/754-3391

■ *WHERE TO STAY*

Black Bart Inn and Motel, *55 St. Charles St. (P.O. Box 576), 209/754-3808; $15.90–$25.44; cribs, pool, TVs in motel rooms.* Here you have a choice of accommodations in the old hotel or in the modern motel.

■ *WHAT TO DO*

Calaveras County Historical Museum, *30 N. Main St., 209/754-4203; in summer M–F 10am–4pm, irregular hours rest of year; adults 50¢, under 13 25¢.* Special items on display in this restored 1867 courthouse include the Murphys Hotel register bearing Mark Twain's signature and an invitation to the 1888 hanging of George W. Cox. A collection of firearms and Indian relics may also be viewed. Courthouse tours occur at 11am, 1, & 3pm.

MOKELUMNE HILL

■ *WHERE TO STAY*

Hotel Leger, *P.O. Box 50, 209/286-1401; $24–$40; cribs, pool, dining facilities.* Once considered one of the most luxurious of Gold Rush hotels, the Hotel Leger has many rooms with sitting areas and fire-places. All are decorated with tasteful old furniture, and the more expensive parlor rooms are quite fancy.

■ *WHERE TO EAT*

Hotel Leger Dining Room, *daily for dinner, brunch on weekends; high-chairs, booster seats, children's portions.* You'll want to sample the delicious sourdough pancakes at brunch. An old-fashioned bar ad-joins the dining room; children can sip sodas through a straw while their parents imbibe something stronger.

JACKSON

Amador County Chamber of Commerce
P.O. Box 596
Jackson 95642
209/223-0350

A booklet, "Gold Fever Panacea," explains the rudiments of goldpanning, including where to purchase equipment and how to file a claim. It is available for 50¢ by mail from the Chamber of Commerce.

■ *SPECIAL EVENTS*

Gold Dust Days, *first part of April.* Participate in free gold panning lessons and field trips. Contact the Chamber of Commerce for details.

Italian Picnic, *first week in June at Italian Picnic Grounds.* The public is invited to this festival which has carnival rides for the kids, dancing for the adults, and a parade in Sutter Creek for everyone.

■ *WHERE TO STAY*

Country Squire Motel, *1105 N. Main St., 209/223-1657; $19.08–$22.26; barbecue area, refrigerator, lawn games, gold panning, includes con-tinental breakfast.* Located out in the country on the site of the old Kennedy Gold Mine, this motel was one of the last private gambling casinos in California. It was closed in 1952. Now some of the units are restored and some have recently been built new. Rooms are decor-ated with antiques. Goldpanning may be practiced year round in the backyard "crick," and ducks and sheep roam freely on the two-acre grounds.

El Campo Casa Resort Motel, *1740 Kennedy Flat Rd., 209/223-0100; $21.50–$32.50; TV, pool, playground, barbecue facilities.* Well-landscaped grounds await you at this motel.

Linda Vista Motel, *1625 N. Hwy 49/Hwy 88, 209/223-1096; $20; cribs, TV.* This is a pleasant Spanish-style motel.

National Hotel, *2 Water St., 209/267-5632, 223-0500; $17.50–$20; Saturday night reservations must include dinner reservations at the hotel.* Claiming to be the oldest hotel in continuous operation (since 1862) in California, the National offers pleasant, clean rooms with private baths.

■ *WHERE TO CAMP*

Lake Amador, *take Hwy 88 west to Jackson Valley Rd., turn left, follow signs through Buena Vista to Lake Amador, 209/274-2625; pool, fishing, picnicking, boating.*

Pardee Reservoir, *take Hoffman Lane/Stony Creek Rd. west for ten miles (Route 1, Box 224, Ione 95640), 209/772-1472; pool, playground, horseback riding, boat rentals, picnicking.*

Roaring Camp, *P.O. Box 278, Pine Grove 95665, 209/296-4100; $180/week for a prospector's cabin.* A four-hour trip to this remote canyon gives you the opportunity to swim in the Mokelumne River, fish, pan for gold, collect rocks, and visit a wildlife museum. On Wednesdays there is a special dinner trip which includes a barbecued steak dinner served on the riverbank under the stars. Campers will stay in rustic cabins and must bring all their gear (except tents). Call for further information and reservations.

■ *WHERE TO EAT*

National Hotel, *highchairs, children's portions.* In this cozy cellar dining room, entrees include a choice of steak, chicken, and fish. Most of the furniture is for sale. If you like the chair you're sitting on, ask the price. Maybe you'll be able to take it home as a souvenir.

Wells Fargo Restaurant, *Water St., 209/223-9956; daily 7am–10pm; highchairs, booster seats.* Daily dinner specials include such items as baked shortribs, roast lamb, roast pork, baked ham, and breaded veal. Well-cooked, generous portions keep locals coming back. Sandwich items are also available at dinner.

Wheel Inn, *1106 N. Main St., 209/223-1008; Tu–Sat 5–10pm, Sun 1–10pm, closed M; highchairs, booster seats, children's portions.* The menu at this family-style restaurant is in the form of a newsletter and includes information about the Kennedy Mine tailing wheels located nearby as well as the promise that the restaurant itself is the "greatest discovery in the Gold Country" and that "big portions of fine food, friendly service, and informal atmosphere have become tradition for thousands of Gold Country residents and visitors." And, indeed, it is a very popular spot.

Wright on Main Ice Cream Parlor, *134 Main, 209/223-0611; daily 11am–5pm; highchairs, booster seats.* Since the turn of the century this old-fashioned ice cream parlor/candy store has been serving up sweet confections. Nowadays you can also enjoy soup, sandwiches, and freshly ground coffee.

■ *WHAT TO DO*

Amador County Museum, *225 Church St., 209/223-2884; Th–M 11:30am–4pm, closed Tu & W; adults $1, 6–12 50¢.* Located inside an 1859 brick home, this museum displays scale models of the Kennedy Mine tailing wheels and head frame and the North Star Mine stamp mill. Their operation is demonstrated on weekends at 1, 2, & 3pm. You can also see primitive medical instruments and a wreath made of human hair.

Roaring Camp, *see page 134.*

Kennedy Mine Tailing Wheels, *on Jackson Gate Rd.* Huge abandoned 58 foot diameter wheels, originally built in 1912 to carry waste gravel from the nearby mine, may be viewed by taking a short walk on well-marked trails.

SUTTER CREEK

■ *A LITTLE BACKGROUND*

Believe it or not, there were once seven gold mines located on this lazy Main Street; now it is filled with antique shops.

■ *WHERE TO EAT*

Bellotti Inn, *53 Main St., 209/267-5211; daily 11:30am–10pm; highchairs, booster seats, children's portions.* Huge Italian family-style dinners are served in this well-established restaurant.

Sutter Creek Palace, *76 Main St., 209/267-9852; Tu–Sun 11am–3pm, 5–9:30pm, closed M; highchairs, booster seats.* The decor here is that of an old western saloon, the walls display antique clocks, and the menu offers gourmet fare. Children should be happy with the always-available hamburger.

VOLCANO

- ## A LITTLE BACKGROUND

Take the scenic route from Sutter Creek—just follow the signs. Because this tiny town is built in a depression on top of limestone caves, it is green year round. Sleepy and quiet now, during the Gold Rush it was well-known for its dance-halls and saloons.

- ## WHERE TO STAY

St. George Hotel, *P.O. Box 275, 95689, 209/296-4458; $22.50, on weekends $30 (includes dinner and breakfast); dining facilities; closed M & Tu and Jan to mid-Feb.* The St. George Hotel offers a choice of rooms in either the main hotel, built in 1862, or in the annex, built almost a hundred years later in 1961. Families with children under 12 are automatically put in the newer annex, their consolation being that they get a private bathroom.

- ## WHERE TO EAT

Jug and Rose Confectionery, *Main St., 209/296-4696; Th–Tu 9am–5pm, closed W, call first, hours change regularly; highchairs, children's portions; breakfast reservations essential.* Famous for their all-you-can-eat breakfasts of sourdough pancakes served with warm spice syrup, sour cream and strawberries, and blackberry topping (whew!), the Jug and Rose has been in business since 1855. The breakfast "special" includes fresh fruit, scrambled eggs, ham, and beverage. Children's pancakes come in animal shapes; parents can choose from a large variety of coffees and teas. Exotic sundaes lure afternoon diners. How about a Moss Rose Sundae (home-made rose petal syrup on vanilla ice cream topped with a real rose), Sierra split (three flavors of ice cream, blackberry topping, and banana), or Buttermilk Skye (a milkshake)? There is a "pint-sized" table and chairs for the kids, and the old oak wallphone located inside this restored Gold Rush saloon really works.

St. George Hotel, *209/296-4458; breakfast and dinner W–Sun, closed M & Tu; highchairs.* Reservations are necessary except on Sunday, when a special chicken dinner is served from 1–6pm.

- ## WHAT TO DO IN TOWN

See the **Cannon.** Located in the center of town in a protected shelter, this cannon—without firing a shot—helped win the Civil War. Cast of bronze and brass in Boston in 1837 and weighing 6 pounds, somehow it reached San Francisco and was smuggled into Volcano in 1863. For the complete story, you'll have to ask around in town.

Park. This is a good spot for the kids to run around and climb some rocks.

Sing Kee's Store, *free.* Built in 1857 and formerly a general store, this building is now a combination museum/trading post.

Volcano Pioneer Community Theater Group, *information: 209/296-7013, reservations: 209/223-3155; F & Sat 8pm curtain, no winter performances; adults $4, special rates for children; reservations necessary.* The first little theater group to form in California was the Volcano Thespian Society in 1854. Children are welcome at performances in the intimate 50-seat theater; indeed, they often are actually on stage in the play.

■ *WHAT TO DO NEARBY*

Daffodil Hill, *located three miles north of town; free.* Originally planted in the 1850s, more than 250 varieties of daffodils bloom here each year from late March through April. Children are sure to enjoy visiting the sheep and chickens penned on the premises.

Indian Grinding Rock

Though there is no admission charge, this is private property, and donations are accepted and seem appropriate. Don't forget your camera. There is a picnic area with tables.

Indian Grinding Rock State Park Historical Monument, *on Pine Grove Rd. southwest of town, 209/296-4440; open daily; $2/car.* The largest of the grinding rocks, a huge flat rock measuring 173 x 82 feet, has over 1,185 mortar holes and 363 rock carvings. All were made by Indians who ground their seed there with pestles. (See photo on page 137.) There is also a Miwok ceremonial roundhouse, a hand-game house, a cultural center, several cedar bark tepees, a grain storage center, an Indian football field, an Indian tepee village, and a nature trail. Special celebrations occur in September. Camping and picnicking facilities are available.

AMADOR CITY

▪ *WHERE TO STAY*

The Mine House, *P.O. Box 226, 95601, 209/267-5900; $31–$36; pool; juice and coffee in morning (kids get hot chocolate).* Authentic antiques furnish the unusual rooms inside this restored brick building, formerly a mine office. In the morning, just push the buzzer and your coffee will be delivered right to the door. One Easter when my family was staying here, we prearranged for an Easter basket to arrive in this same mysterious manner. Our son still hasn't figured out how that one was pulled off.

▪ *WHERE TO EAT*

Buffalo Chips Emporium, *Hwy 49, 209/267-0570; daily 9am–5pm.* You can buy a cone here and then sit outside on one of the old benches and leisurely watch the busy world go by. If you try, you can almost imagine the cars are really horses in disguise. Breakfast and lunch are also served inside this old-fashioned ice cream parlor.

The Cellar, *Hwy 49, 209/267-0384; Tu, Th–Sun lunch and dinner, closed M & W.* The specialties here are fondue, crepes, and sandwiches made with homemade sourdough bread. Children can look forward to "The Minor," a peanut butter and jelly sandwich. Chocolate fondue and pastries are available for dessert.

DRYTOWN

■ *A LITTLE BACKGROUND*
Once the home of 26 saloons, Drytown is now known for its equally abundant antique shops.

■ *WHAT TO DO*
Piper Playhouse, *209/245-3812; Sat 8:30pm curtain, May–Sept; $6/person; reservations necessary.* Enjoy a raucous melodrama. Call for current schedule.

SHINGLE SPRINGS

■ *WHERE TO EAT*
Sam's Town, *Hwy 50/Cameron Park, 95682, 916/677-2273, 933-1662; daily 6am–2am.* This is a funky combination restaurant/honky-tonk piano bar/general store/memorabilia museum. The outside is littered with covered wagons and the inside floors with peanut shells discarded by happy revelers. There is also an arcade of nickelodeons and pinball machines. This makes an ideal stop for a snack, and you can choose from hamburgers, fried chicken, or prime rib and champagne.

■ *WHERE TO CAMP*
Crazy Horse Campgrounds, *P.O. Box 388, 95682, 916/677-2258; $7.50–$9/night; gold panning, 350 ft. water slide, swimming, boating, fishing, kiddie rides, playground, miniature golf, recreation hall, horseback riding.* Call or write for the current "special events" schedule. Something special—aloha weekend, bathtub regatta, Oktoberfest, wagon train days—always seems to be happening. Children should be thrilled about taking the raft to Tom Sawyer Island, hitching a ride on the firetruck, and hiding in the two tree forts.

EL DORADO

■ *WHERE TO EAT*
Poor Red's, *Hwy 49, 916/622-2901; lunch M–F 11:30am–2pm, dinner M–Sat 5–10pm, Sun 2–10pm; highchairs, booster seats.* Hams, ribs, chicken, and steak are all cooked over an open oakwood pit and served in generous portions. Because it is very popular and also small,

weekend dinner waits can be as long as 1–2 hours. If you're prepared, you can possibly enjoy that time downing *Gold Cadillacs* at the old-fashioned horseshoe-shaped bar. If you don't want a long wait, go for lunch or get an order to take out.

PLACERVILLE

El Dorado County Chamber of Commerce
P.O. Box 268
(542 Main St.)
Placerville 95667
916/626-2344

Hangtown Chamber of Commerce
P.O. Box 151
(464 Main St.)
Placerville 95667
916/622-5611

■ *SPECIAL EVENTS*
Reenactment of Pony Express, *July in Pollock Pines, 916/644-3970.*

■ *A LITTLE BACKGROUND*
Placerville was once known as Hangtown, because hangings were so common. This is where the Hangtown Fry (eggs, bacon, and oysters) originated. Mark Hopkins, Philip Armour, and John Studebaker all got their financial starts here as well.

■ *WHERE TO EAT*
John Pearson Soda Works & Bottling Room, *594 Main St.; downstairs: 916/622-4840, upstairs: 916/626-3528; highchairs.* Limestone cooling caves are still in the back and old-fashioned furniture and glassware are still in use in this old-time (circa 1850) soda fountain and candy shop (daily noon–9pm). Diners get upstairs, where continental dinners are served, via a water-powered elevator or old iron staircase (W–Sun 5–9pm).

■ *WHAT TO DO IN TOWN*
Bedford Park/Gold Bug Mine, *on Bedford Ave., 916/622-0832; daily 8:30am–dusk; free.* Visitors can walk through the ¼-mile long lighted mine shaft, picnic, or hike in this rugged 68-acre park.

El Dorado County Historical Museum, *El Dorado County Fairgrounds, 916/626-2250; W–Sat 10am–4pm, Sun noon–3:30pm; free.* See an old stagecoach—and a wheelbarrow made in 1853 by John Studebaker, who went on to manufacture cars.

Mama's Llamas, *see page 180.*

- ## WHAT TO DO NEARBY

  Apple Hill. Located on a mountain ridge east of town, the route for the Apple Hill tour follows a historic path originally blazed out in 1857 by Pony Express riders. The various member farms along this route will sell you tree-fresh apples at bargain prices as well as homemade apple foods. Picnic facilities, hiking trails, fishing ponds, pony rides, and train rides are also available. For a free map to the farms send a legal size stamped, self-addressed envelope to: Apple Hill, P.O. Box 494, Camino 95709.

  Sutter Gaslight Theater, *720 Sutter St., Folsom 95630 (28 miles east of town on Hwy 50), 916/985-4510; F & Sat 8:30pm curtain; $5/person; reservations necessary.* The whole family is urged to boo, hiss, and cheer the melodrama being presented. A vaudeville show is included.

GEORGETOWN

- ## WHERE TO STAY

  The Georgetown Hotel, *P.O. Box 187, 95634, 916/333-4373; $20–$30; dining facilities for lunch and dinner.* This restored Victorian hotel offers no private baths, but you will have shared access to a seven-foot long clawfoot tub.

COLOMA

- ## A LITTLE BACKGROUND

  This is where gold was first discovered in California in 1848 by James Marshall. The 220-acre state park encompasses 70% of the town.

- ## WHERE TO STAY

  Camp Coloma, *P.O. Box 11, 916/622-6700; $18.50; pony wagon, horses, children's animal farm, pool, playground, fishing pond, gold panning, raft trips.* These modern cabins are located on the American River. Campsites are also available.

Sierra Nevada House III, *P.O. Box 268, 95613, 916/622-5856; $26.50; cribs, includes breakfast.* An authentic reconstruction built nearby the ruins of two former hotels of the same name (they burned in 1907 and 1926), Sierra Nevada House III features a soda fountain,

Where the Gold Rush began: reconstruction of the original Sutter sawmill.

dispensing inexpensive meals and a soda made from an 80-year-old recipe, and a dining room, where you can get delicious homemade dinners with all the trimmings. If food was this good here during the Gold Rush, the miners must have lost plenty of gold while they sat here eating instead of panning. The breakfast is a hearty meal of flapjacks, orange juice, and coffee.

■ *WHERE TO CAMP*

Camp Lotus, *P.O. Box 578 (two miles from town), Lotus 95651, 916/ 622-8672.* This lovely campground, located on the American River, has facilities for river swimming, nature walks, volleyball, horseshoes, and fishing.

■ *WHAT TO DO*

Marshall Gold Discovery State Historic Park, *916/622-3470; daily 10am– 5pm; $1.50/car; museum: adults 50¢, under 18 free.* This reconstruction of the original Sutter sawmill—where the Gold Rush began—is now a lovely picnic area with hiking trails and a museum. The mill operates on weekends at 2pm.

AUBURN

Auburn Chamber of Commerce
1101 High St.
Auburn 95603
916/885-5616
Contact the above for a free historic guide to Old Town, map of Hwy 49, and/or street map of Auburn.

Placer County Chamber of Commerce
661 Newcastle Rd.
Newcastle 95658
916/663-2061

■ *WHERE TO STAY*

Motel Row. There are a number of modern motels located on Lincoln Way. Just drive there, and take your pick.

■ *WHERE TO EAT*

Auburn Drug Store, *815 Lincoln Way, 916/885-6524; M–Sat 9am–6pm, closed Sun.* The soda fountain in this old drug store dispenses phosphates and sodas as well as an old-time atmosphere that is rapidly becoming extinct.

Auburn Hotel, *853 Lincoln Way, 916/885-8132; dinners daily.* The Basque/Italian menu features nightly specials. Call for the current menu.

The Butterworth, *1522 Lincoln Way, 916/885-0249; Tu–Sat 11am–2pm, 5–9pm, Sun 11am–2:30pm, closed M; reservations essential.* The historic Brye Mansion, restored now to its Victorian gingerbread splendor, houses three dining rooms and features English and continental cuisine. Some of the unusual Sunday brunch items you will encounter are steak & kidney pie, Dorchester steak, Danish egg puffs, and Alaskan avocado.

■ *WHAT TO DO*

Gold Rush Plaza Old Opera House Dinner Theater, *111 Sacramento St., 916/885-7708; F & Sat 8:30pm curtain, dinner served at 7:30pm; adults: $6/dinner, $5/entertainment, children: ½ price for dinner only.* Various melodramas are staged here to bring back some good old-fashioned entertainment. Dinners are served in the theater before showtime. You may see just the play if you wish. Call for further details and reservations.

Placer County Historical Museum, *1273 High St., Gold Country fairgrounds, 916/885-9570; daily 10am–4pm; free.* Here you will see a reconstruction of an old kitchen, dining room, bedroom, and parlor as well as some birds eggs and nests and a variety of weapons.

GRASS VALLEY

Grass Valley Chamber of Commerce
106 S. Auburn
Grass Valley 95945
916/273-4667

■ *SPECIAL EVENTS*

Bluegrass Festival, *in June.*

■ *A LITTLE BACKGROUND*

There's really not much to do in Grass Valley but relax. I find it to be a nice stop on the first night out visiting the northern Gold Rush country. The drive along country roads is scenic and should be relished during daylight hours rather than being passed through quickly in a mad, after-dark dash for sleeping accommodations.

■ WHERE TO STAY

Alta Sierra Motel, *135 Tammy Way/across from the Alta Sierra Country Club, 916/273-9102; $26; TV.* Located down a winding country road, finding this rustic modern motel is like going on a treasure hunt. Just keep following those signs and when you find the motel, you'll probably agree that it's somewhat of a treasure. Located on spacious picturesque grounds, it overlooks a small lake. The room interiors are woodsy and spacious and not at all run-of-the-mill. A country club is located across the street; you may use the pool, golf course, and inexpensive restaurant serving breakfast and lunch.

Gold Country Inn, *11972 Sutton Way, 916/273-1393; $20–$26; TV, pool, some kitchens.*

Golden Chain Resort Motel, *13363 Hwy 49, 916/273-7279; $20–$30; TV, pool, putting green, dining facilities.*

Sivananda Ashram Vrindavan Yoga Farm, *P.O. Box 795, 916/273-9802; $15/person.* The bell rings at 5:30 each morning to wake guests here. Attendance at the scheduled meditation and yoga disciplines is mandatory. In between, guests are fed vegetarian meals and given plenty of free time to enjoy the natural surroundings of the 60-acre farm. For sleeping there is a separate men's and women's dorm as well as small huts for couples and families. At these rates you shouldn't mind bringing your own sleeping bags. Beginners to yoga are welcome, as are children.

■ WHERE TO EAT

King Richard's Pasties, *251 S. Auburn, 916/273-0286; M–F 9am–6:30pm, Sat 9:30am–6pm, closed Sun.* This unusual takeout eatery specializes in pasties—an English dough treat. How about a tasty pasty picnic?

Scheidel's Old European Restaurant, *Hwy 49 six miles south of town, 916/273-5553; W–Sat 5:30–10pm, Sun 4–9pm, closed M & Tu; children's portions; reservations suggested.* European and Swiss cuisine are featured fare at this charming and popular spot.

Tofanelli's, *302 W. Main St., 916/273-9927; open daily; highchairs, booster seats.* Originally a grocery store and then a meat market, Tofanelli's is now a great place to go for breakfast. The airy interior and oak decor make a pleasant background in which to enjoy such delicacies as whole wheat pancakes and waffles, a variety of omelettes, and homemade chocolate chip, pumpkin, or orange muffins.

■ *WHAT TO DO*

Empire Mine State Historic Park, *338 Empire St., Central Park, 916/273-8522; daily 9am–5pm; adults 50¢.* Guided tours of the grounds and gardens are available in the summer, as are movies and ranger-led talks. A self-guiding tour is available at other times.

Lola Montez's Home, *Mill St.; daily in summer noon–4pm; free.* You can learn more about this well-known Gold Rush personality when you tour her former home.

Memorial Park, *916/273-3171.* This is a good spot to picnic, get in a game of tennis, swim in the public pool or creek, or let the kids have some fun at the playground.

Mount St. Mary's Museum, *S. Church/Chapel Sts., 916/273-4103; daily noon–3pm; 50¢.* Formerly the 1865 Mount Saint Mary's convent, this building now displays Gold Rush furnishings as well as a fully equipped doctor's office and classroom from that era.

North Star Mine Power House Museum, *Lower Mill St./Empire, 916/273-9853; daily in summer 11am–5pm, in winter 10am–4pm and closed W & Th; adults 50¢, under 18 free.* Some say this is the best museum in the Gold Country. Housed in the lovely former North Star Mine Powerhouse is a collection of old photographs, mining dioramas and models, and 30 foot Felton water wheels weighing ten tons each. There is a grassy picnic area across Wolf Creek.

NEVADA CITY

Nevada City Chamber of Commerce
132 Main St.
Nevada City 95959
916/265-2692

■ *SPECIAL EVENTS*

Home Tour, *in May and October.* Contact the Chamber of Commerce for further information.

■ *WHERE TO STAY IN TOWN*

The National Hotel, *211 Broad St., 916/265-4551; $23.10–$30.45; cribs, pool, dining facilities.* Claiming to be the oldest continuously operated hotel in the West, this quiet hotel looks much as it did when it was built in 1856. It is funished with authentic Victorian antiques, but the roof-top swimming pool and indoor plumbing are concessions to modern comfort.

Northern Queen Motel, *400 Railroad Ave., 916/265-5824; $21–$25.20; pool, jacuzzi, TV.*

■ *WHERE TO STAY NEARBY*

Herrington's Sierra Pines, *P.O. Box 235, Sierra City 96125, 916/862-1151; $26–$35; TV, balconies, cottage with kitchen and fireplace, dining facilities.* Located on the north fork of the Yuba River, this motel has a pond where you can fish for trout. The restaurant is known for its fresh rainbow trout and baked goods.

Kenton Mine Lodge & Cookhouse, *located off Hwy 49, 45 miles north of Nevada City (P.O. Box 942), Alleghany 95910, 916/287-3212; $60–$70; includes three meals, cribs.* Each day three homemade meals are served family-style at long communal tables, encouraging interaction with other guests. Informal evening entertainment includes campfires. Lodging is a choice of creekside cabins or private rooms in the restored miners' boarding house—all originally built in the 1930s. During the day guests may borrow gold pans to try their skill, take a hike, explore the abandoned mine, fish for trout, and wade in the creek. If you plan to visit just for a meal, call ahead for reservations.

Malakoff Diggins State Historic Park, *see page 148.*

Sierra Shangri-la, *P.O. Box 285, Downieville 95936, 916/289-3455; $30–$39; cribs, decks, kitchens.* There is little to do at Shangri-la except commune with nature. Relax, do some fishing and hiking, and enjoy the sights and sounds of the Yuba River rushing past your cottage door.

WHERE TO CAMP
Oregon Creek, *see page 150.*

WHERE TO EAT
American Victorian Museum Restaurant, *325 Spring St., 916/265-5804; F 6-9pm, Sat noon-2pm, 6-9pm, Sun 10:30am-2pm; highchairs, children's portions.* You won't want to miss having a meal in this cavernous hall which also houses an interesting museum and performance area. Crepes, omelettes, and avocado enchiladas are on the menu along with homemade bread and desserts. Sunday brunch features a buffet; dinner features an a la carte continental menu.

Cafe Les Stace, *311 Broad, 916/265-6440; daily 8am-3pm, 5-9pm; highchairs, booster seats.* Omelettes are available for both breakfast and lunch; Mexican food is featured at dinner. The fresh, tasty food is accented with mellow background music.

Creeky Pete's Garden Cafe, *300 Commercial, 916/265-6951; Tu-Sun 9am-9pm, closed M; highchairs, booster seats.* The lunch and dinner menus are the same and offer salads, sandwiches, crepes, desserts, and snacks. The indoor area is beautifully decorated with oak furniture and green plants. The outdoor area is protected from the elements with huge umbrellas and colorfully decorated with blooming flowers. Occasionally there is live guitar music for entertainment.

Friar Tuck's, *111 N. Pine, 916/265-2262; W-Sun 5-10:30pm; children's portions.* This is the place to go if you enjoy fondue.

National Hotel, *211 Broad St., 916/265-2348; open daily; children's portions.* Dinners are expensive and fancy here. Breakfast, lunch, and the ten-course Sunday brunch are more casual and more suitable for families.

The Soda Saloon, *Broad/N. Pine, 916/265-5504; M-F 6am-6pm, weekends 7am-7pm; highchairs.* Here you can choose from over 25 soda flavors. If you can't make up your mind, try the "Green River," a lemon-lime drink. Breakfast and lunch items are also on the menu.

WHAT TO DO
Bridgeport Bridge, *take Hwy 49 north, then left on Pleasant Valley Rd.* Built in 1862 and in use until 1971, this is the longest (233 feet) wood-covered bridge in the west. It is now a California state historical landmark.

Malakoff Diggins State Historic Park, *take Hwy 49 17 miles northeast of town, at 23579 North Bloomfield/Graniteville Rd., North Bloomfield 95959; daily April-Sept 10am-5pm, weekends rest of year; free.* Once inhabited by over 1,500 people and a center for the hydraulic mining operation, North Bloomfield is now a ghost town. Several

buildings have been restored, a supplies shop features a clerk in period dress, but there are no commercial stores. The park Historic Center has an interpretive display on hydraulic mining. On weekends at 2pm there is a demonstration of an old hydraulic mining monitor followed by a tour of the town. Old logging roads make for good hiking, a small lake is stocked with fish, and there are picnic facilities. Camp-sites are available through Ticketron (see page 192), and two "rustic" cabins may be rented through the park.

Nevada County Historical Society Museums:

American Victorian Museum, *325 Spring St., 916/265-5804; daily 10am–4pm; by donation.* The American Victorian Museum is located in the historic Miners Foundry, where machine parts and architectural iron were once manufactured for use throughout the world. It is the only museum in the United States devoted to collecting, preserving and exhibiting art and artifacts from the Victorian period (1840–1900). Acting as a cultural center for the community, the museum hosts theater productions, concerts, and lectures in its huge Old Stone Hall—one of the largest free-span rooms of its kind in the area. Call for the current calendar of events.

Firehouse Museum, *Main/Commercial Sts., 916/265-9941; daily 11am–4pm; by donation.* Located inside an 1861 firehouse, this museum is said to be haunted. Come here to see a Chinese altar and snowshoes for a horse, among other things. Even more pioneer memorabilia may be found in the annex **Bicentennial Museum.**

Martin Luther Marsh House, *254 Boulder St., 916/265-5804; weekend guided tours May–Oct, 1 & 2:15pm; $1.50; reservations suggested.* The tour of this completely restored and authentically furnished Victorian Italianate house, built in 1873, allows you to see *all* the rooms.

Nevada Theatre, *401 Broad St., 916/265-6161; usually F & Sat evenings; $4–$7.50/person.* Opened in July 1865, this claims to be the oldest theater building in California. It was recently refurbished to look as it did when it first opened. There are sometimes movies on winter Sunday afternoons. Call for information on the current production.

Oregon Creek Swimming Hole, *18 miles north of town on Hwy 49.* Located on the middle fork of the Yuba River, this area has sandy beaches, deep swimming and shallow wading spots, and picnic facilities. A Tahoe National Forest campground is also located here.

Rubbings, *212 Main, 916/265-6111.* The first shop of its kind in the United States, this interesting business specializes in brass rubbings. Some are already done and ready to purchase; others are waiting for you to do yourself. A special child's kit (good for beginning adults too) includes waxes, scissors, and papers. The proprietor is eager to help and answer any questions you might have about this old art form.

LAKE TAHOE

SOUTH LAKE TAHOE

South Lake Tahoe Visitor's Bureau
P.O. Box 15090
South Lake Tahoe 95702
toll-free 800/822-5977 (reservations service, weather and road conditions)
toll-free 800/648-5450 (information)

- *A LITTLE BACKGROUND*
Lake Tahoe lies half in California and half in Nevada. It is the largest (193 sq. miles surface) and deepest (1645 feet) lake in North America and the second-largest alpine lake in the world. At 6,225 feet above sea level, in the summer its waters are a crystal clear deep blue and make a striking contrast with the extensive green forests and majestic mountains encircling it. Once a remote Sierra lake, Tahoe is now a popular and well-equipped vacation area offering a wide range of recreational activities as well as spectacular scenery. Swimming, hiking, boating, tennis, bicycling, horseback riding, river rafting, camping, fishing, water-skiing, and backpacking are some of the summer outdoor activities you can look forward to. In winter, of course, there is excellent skiing. On the Nevada side gambling is another big attraction. You may bring your

children into a casino to go to a restaurant, but note that children are not allowed to "loiter or play" the slot machines—not even babies in backpacks.

- **ROUTE**
Located approximately 200 miles north of San Francisco. Take Hwy 80 to Hwy 50 to the lake.

- **STOPS ALONG THE WAY**
The Nut Tree, *see page 104.*
Poor Red's, *see page 139.*
Sacramento, *see page 103.*
Sam's Town, *see page 139.*

- **CHILDCARE**
Harrah's Casino has a "varsity lounge" for children 6–17 who are at least 46 inches tall. The admission charge is $1.50 and there is a four hour maximum. The lounge has ping-pong, pool tables, bowling, jukeboxes, a movie theater, kiddie rides, TV, and a snack bar. Sure beats sitting on the curb reading comic books like I did when I was a kid. For further information and hours call toll-free 800/648-3773 or 702/588-6611 x447. In the past Harrah's has had a nursery for children age 2–6. Call to confirm its current status.

Lake Tahoe Day Camp has trained counselors, all age 25 or older, who will take children age 5–14 on all-day field trips around the area. Activities include swimming, fishing, and hiking. Lunch and snacks are included. For reservations and information contact Lake Tahoe Day Camp, P.O. Box 13760, South Lake Tahoe, CA 95702, 916/544-CAMP.

Childcare Centers which take drop-ins are:
A-1 Children's Center South, *1931 D St., 916/541-4688.*
Heavenly Baby Care, *3624 Needle Peak Rd., 916/544-6323.*
Humpty Dumpty Child Care Center, *3572 Bill Ave., 916/544-2952.*
Kindertown, *2249 Helen Ave., 916/541-7310.*
Tiny Piny Preschool, *Pioneer Trail/Tamarack Ave., 916/544-5444.*
Always call first to be sure there is space available and to determine hours, prices, and ages.

- **WHERE TO STAY**
CONDOS:
Accommodation Station, *P.O. Box 14441, 916/541-2355; $42 and up.*

Privately-owned condominiums, cabins, and homes may be rented through this agency. Price is determined by how many bedrooms your party needs and what type of accommodation you choose.

Lakeland Village, *P.O. Box 8, 95705, 916/541-7711, toll-free reservations 800/822-5969; $52–$72, packages available; 2 tennis courts (fee), color TV, kitchens, 2 pools, wading pool, jacuzzi, sauna, recreation room, fireplaces, playground, casino shuttle bus, some lake views.* Although it is located on bustling Hwy 50, Lakeland Village still manages to retain a secluded, restive feeling. The luxury condominiums are spacious and comfortable and have most of the comforts of home. Many of the units are located right on the lake; all are within a few minutes walk.

LAKEFRONT:

Royal Vahalla Motor Lodge, *Drawer GG, 95729, 916/544-2233; $25–$46; cribs, pool, color TV, some balconies and lakeviews.*

Sail-In Motel Apartments, *861 Lakeview Ave. (P.O. Box 653), 95705, 916/544-8615; $35; TV, some lakeviews and kitchens.* Located off the beaten path, this attractive and comfortable motel is close to a park.

Tahoe Marina Inn, *P.O. Box 871, 95705, 916/541-2180; $30–$55; cribs, sauna, private beach, pool, some kitchens and lakeviews.* Located on the edge of the lake, the majority of the rooms here have lakeviews. There are also some beachside condominiums with fireplaces ($64–$69).

Timber Cove Lodge, *Hwy 50/Johnson Blvd. (P.O. Box AC), 95705, 916/541-6722, toll-free reservations 800/528-1234; $48; cribs, pool, casino transportation, private beach, marina, pier, color TV, dining facilities.*

■ *WHERE TO STAY NEARBY*

Zephyr Cove Resort, *on Hwy 50 approximately four miles north of Stateline (P.O. Box 199), Zephyr Cove, Nevada 89448, 702/588-6644, 588-6645; rooms $12.50–$16, cabins $21 and up; cribs, private beach, casino, recreation center, boat rentals, stables, dining facilities.* Located in a lovely forested area by the lake, these rustic cabins and inexpensive lodge rooms provide a convenient yet out-of-the-way spot to stay. Tennis courts are nearby, and it is only a short drive to casino-packed Stateline. Campsites are also available ($4–$8).

■ *WHERE TO CAMP*

Tahoe Valley Campground, *P.O. Box 9026, 95731, 916/541-2222, 541-3700; stables.*

U.S. Forest Service, *call the Lake Tahoe Visitor's Center 916/544-6420 for a brochure listing the area's campgrounds.*

Zephyr Cove, *see page 153.*

■ WHERE TO EAT

Casinos. For some of the best and least expensive food in this area, try the casino restaurants. Most offer bargain prices and family accommodations. My favorites are:

Harvey's Pancake Parlor, *24 hours a day; highchairs and booster seats.* Breakfast isn't the only meal to come here for. Dinner features delicious, bargain-priced entrees of southern fried chicken and New York steak.

Sahara Tahoe Bonanza Buffet, *916/588-6211; daily 5–11pm, weekend brunch 9am–2pm.* This huge buffet is sure to satisfy even the hungriest customer. Each evening features a different theme.

Cantina Los Tres Hombres, *Hwy 89/10th St. (¼ mile north of the "Y"); daily 5–10pm; highchairs, children's portions; no reservations.* Anticipate a wait of at least one hour at this popular spot, but don't let it stop you. We sit in the bar and order a pitcher of Margaritas for the adults, some soft drinks for the kids, and some nachos (tortilla chips heated with green chiles, melted cheese, chorizo, and topped with sour cream and guacamole) for everyone. Then we settle into the noisy, happy surroundings and munch and sip. We often find that our hunger is satisfied after so indulging, and we are ready to leave before we are even called to a table. When we do stick around to dine, we favor ordering one of the huge burritos stuffed with a variety of tasty fillings.

The Cook Book, *787 Emerald Bay Rd., 916/541-8400; daily 7:30am–10pm; highchairs, booster seats; no reservations.* Claiming to have the largest omelette menu on earth, the Cook Book also has what may be the longest wait. While you're waiting, get a copy of the menu and begin to decide which omelette you want to try from among the hundreds of possibilities. For those of you who are hard to please, the usual breakfast, lunch, dinner items are also available.

Top of the Tram, *Heavenly Valley, 916/544-6263; daily for dinner 5–11pm, Sunday brunch 10am–2pm; tramride included with brunch only.* A bright red aerial tram carries you 2,000 feet above Lake Tahoe to a family-style dinner featuring a choice of prime rib, rack of lamb, and stuffed trout. Try to dine before dark so that you can enjoy the magnificent views and sunset. If you're not hungry, the tram ride alone is $4.50 for adults and $3.00 for children 12 and under.

■ WHAT TO DO

AMUSEMENT CENTERS:

Magic Carpet Golf, *2455 Hwy 50, 916/541-3787; two 19-hole miniature golf courses.*

Stateline Amusement, *4050 Hwy 50, 916/541-1474; arcade, 19-hole miniature golf course.*

Tahoe Amusement Park, *2401 Hwy 50, 916/541-1300; kiddie rides, giant slide.*

Angora Lakes. Take the road to Fallen Leaf (visit the lake there to see the falls) and turn left at the sign to Angora Lakes. It is a mile hike from the end of the road to the lakes, where you should be able to find a quiet spot to picnic and swim.

BICYCLE RENTALS:

Anderson's Bicycle Rental, *3131 Harrison Ave., 916/541-0500.*

Little Switzerland, *Hwy 50/Navahoe, Tahoe Paradise, 916/577-5646.*

For a map of Tahoe biking trails contact: South Lake Tahoe Recreation Department, 1180 Rufus Allen Blvd., 916/541-4611.

BOATING:

Lake Tahoe Cruises, *located at Ski Run Marina at the base of Ski Run Blvd., 916/541-4652; two-hour trips to Emerald Bay leave daily at 11:15am, 1:15, & 3:15pm; adults $5, 12–15 $4.50, 2–11 $4.*

Lake Tahoe Sailboat Charter Co., *2435 Venice Dr., 916/541-5053; guided cruises, sailing lessons, rentals.*

Miss Tahoe Cruises, *located at Lakeside Marina at foot of Park Ave. (P.O. Box 14292); 916/541-4652; daily two-hour cruises to Emerald Bay leave at 11am, 1:30, and 3:30pm, sunset cruise at 6:30; adults $7, children $3.50.*

M.S. Dixie, *Drawer 830, Zephyr Cove, Nevada 89448, 702/588-3508, 916/541-6617; daily cruises to Emerald Bay leave at 11am & 2pm; adults $6.50, under 12 $4.* Lunch is available on board. Dinner cruises featuring New York steaks, California wines, and dancing leave daily at 5pm (adults $15, under 12 $8.75). Call for reservations.

Rentals, *Timber Cove Marina, 916/544-2942.* Canoes, kayaks, paddleboats, and more are available for rent. Water skiing instruction is also available.

Woodwind, *Zephyr Cove Pier, Nevada, 702/588-3000; adults $5, under 12 $4.* Rides on this 41 foot trimaran leave three times each day. A sunset cruise, including champagne and hors d'oeuvres, is also available ($10/person). Call for departure times.

Drive Around the Lake. A leisurely drive around the 72-mile perimeter of Lake Tahoe can be accomplished in about 2½ hours. Allow extra time, though, as there are many tempting places to stop for picnicking, resting, swimming, and exploring.

Grover Hot Springs, *located approximately 20 miles southeast in Grover Hot Springs State Park, 916/694-2248; $1/person.* Beautifully situated in a valley meadow ringed by pine-covered slopes, these springs are nonsulfurous. Two concrete pools are available—a 102° small one and an 80° larger one. They are well-maintained, clean, safe, and lifeguards are on duty. This is a popular aprés ski destination in the winter.

HORSEBACK RIDING:

Camp Richardson Corral and Pack Station, *916/541-3113; breakfast rides, Sunday brunch ride, barbecue dinner ride, regular guided rides, fishing trips, overnight pack trips, spot pack trips; no children under 6; reservations necessary.*

Stateline Stables, *916/541-9896; horse rentals, hayrides.*

Tahoe Valley Campgrounds Stables, *916/541-2222*

Lake Tahoe Visitor Center, *Hwy 89 north of Camp Richardson, 916/ 544-0209; daily in summer 9am–6pm.* Enjoy campfire programs, guided nature tours, self-guided trails, and Taylor Creek Stream Profile Chamber (underground viewing of mountain stream life).

Lake Tahoe Historical Society Log Cabin Museum, *Star Lake Ave. off Hwy 50; daily in summer 11am–4pm.* See interesting memorabilia of Tahoe's history. You can also pick up a self-guided tour map to 20 historic sites located around the lake.

Tahoe Drive-In, *on Glenwood Way, 916/541-2121; daily.* Movies begin at dusk. Call for current schedule.

Tahoe Trout Farm, *1203 Blue Lake Ave. off Hwy 50, 916/544-0761; daily 9am–6pm; charged by size of fish caught, cleaning extra.* Though there is, of course, no challenge to catching trout here, there are some compelling reasons to give it a try. No license is required, and there is no limit. Bait and tackle are furnished free. You are virtually guaranteed to go home with tasty fare for dinner. Young children, who frustrate easily, are sure to succeed at catching a fish. Do bear in mind, however, that some children will be appalled at the idea of eating the fish they catch.

Top of the Tram, *see page 154.*

Vikingsholm, *reached by a scenic one-mile walk from the parking area on Hwy 89 in Emerald Bay.* The Lake Tahoe Visitor Center offers daily guided tours (916/544-6420). Many boat cruises pass close enough to this 1929 granite and wood castle for a view from the water.

Winter Activities, *see page 183.*

SIDE TRIP:

VIRGINIA CITY

Virginia City Visitors Bureau
South C St.
Virginia City, Nevada 89440
702/847-0177
A short film on the city's history is shown here continuously every day.

■ *SPECIAL EVENTS*

Camel Races, *in September.* Contact the Reno Chamber of Commerce for details (see page 166).

■ *A LITTLE BACKGROUND*

After the quiet, scenic drive through the hills from Lake Tahoe, arrival in Virginia City—with its noisy beerhalls and gaudy signs—can be a bit shocking to the senses. Touted as "the liveliest ghost town in the old west," it certainly does seem to exude a honky-tonk atmosphere.

An authentic western mining town, Virginia City's main street is lined with shops, museums, and saloons. Many of the old Victorian mansions have been restored and are open to the public. On the outskirts of town is an interesting graveyard. Take time to read the epitaphs, and be sure to bring your camera.

The favored cuisine in town is hot dogs and cold beer. Dessert is at its best at the ice cream parlor or candy shop.

■ *ROUTE*

Driving time is approximately 45 minutes. Take Hwy 50 east through Carson City to Hwy 17 north. Follow the signs to Virginia City.

■ **WHERE TO EAT**

Julia Bulette Saloon and Supper House, *South C St., 702/847-9991.* The specialty of the house is pizza with a wholewheat crust.

The Sharon House, *Taylor/C Sts., 702/847-0133; daily 5–11pm.* Located inside the old Bank of California building, this restaurant serves generous portions of Chinese and American food. Drinks may be enjoyed at an antique bar.

■ **WHAT TO DO**

The Castle; *daily May–Oct 10am–5pm; adults $1, under 13 25¢.* Built in 1868, this house is furnished with antiques and open to the public.

Chinatown, *three blocks down the hill from the Bucket of Blood Saloon on Union St.; daily noon-dusk; adults $1, children free.* This recreation of Chinatown features 12 miniature buildings including a fish market, opium den, laundry, and herb shop—all authentically furnished and staffed with mannequins.

Chollar Mine, *South F St., 702/847-0155; daily tours April–Oct 11am–6pm; adults $2, 6–16 $1.* This is a combination gold and silver mine.

Virginia and Truckee Railroad, *located between D and F Sts. (P.O. Box 467), 702/847-0380; daily May–Sept 10:30am–6pm; adults $2.25, 5–12 $1.* This railroad originally carried miners into Carson City and ran as many as 45 trains a day. Now the steam engine carries passengers on a 1½ mile trip to Gold Hill, currently a ghost town. Traveling in open cars or in the restored caboose, passengers enjoy the scenic desert hills and get occasional glimpses of an abandoned mine.

NORTH LAKE TAHOE

North Lake Tahoe Chamber of Commerce
P.O. Box 884
(950 N. Lake Blvd.)
Tahoe City 95730
916/583-2371

North Tahoe Convention Bureau Reservations Service
916/583-3494

■ *GETTING THERE*

You can also get here by train. The Chicago-bound Amtrak train leaves Oakland at 1:15pm and makes six stops before disembarking passengers in Truckee at 6:45pm. Call toll-free

800/648-3850 for fare and schedule information and to make reservations.

■ *ROUTE*

Take Hwy 80 to Truckee, then Hwy 267 south to the lake.

■ *CHILDCARE*

Animal Crackers, *380 Pioneer Way, Tahoe City, 916/583-1058; M–F 7:30am–6pm, Sat & Sun 8am–5pm; ages 2–8.* Drop-in care is available by appointment in this nursery school.

Children's House, *2810 Lake Forest Rd., Lake Forest, 916/583-1636; M–F 7:30am–6pm, weekends 10am–4pm, evenings 6–10pm; ages 2½–6.* Drop-in care is available by reservation in the summer day camp program.

The Chamber of Commerce maintains a list of registered sitters.

■ *WHERE TO STAY*

Last-minute lodging can often be found among the numerous motels and cabins lining the lake in Kings Beach and Tahoe Vista. Your chances are best, of course, during the week.

The Tahoe Escape (3000 N. Lake Blvd. [P.O. Box UU], Tahoe City 95730, 916/583-0151) is a computer reservation system for condominium rentals on the north and west shores.

LAKE FRONT MOTELS:

Agate Bay Lodge, *6565 N. Lake Blvd., Tahoe Vista 95732, 916/546-2788; $26–$36; pool, sauna, private beach, color TV, cribs, barbecue area, ping pong, some kitchens and cottages.*

Beesley's Cottages, *6674 N. Lake Blvd. (P.O. Box 47), Tahoe Vista 95732, 916/546-2448; $39; private beach, playground.*

The Dunes Resort, *P.O. Box 34, Tahoe Vista 95732, 916/546-2196; $26–$39; TV, private beach, recreational facilities, some cottages.*

James Lakeshore Resort, *6834 N. Lake Blvd. (P.O. Box 77), Tahoe Vista, 916/546-9924; $32–$50; private beach, some cottages and kitchens.*

The Trading Post Resort, *5240 N. Lake Blvd. (P.O. Box 331), Carnelian Bay 95711, 916/546-2652; $40; TV, cribs, fireplaces, pier, sundeck, swings, some cabins and kitchens.*

Villa Vista Resort, *6750 N. Lake Blvd. (P.O. Box 85), Tahoe Vista 95732, 916/546-3518; $28–$33; pool, private beach, color TV, playground, barbecues, kayak rentals, some cottages and kitchens.*

Hyatt Lake Tahoe Casino, *P.O. Box 3239, Incline Village, Nevada 89450, 702/831-1111, toll-free reservations 800/228-9000.* A special mid-week package costing just $99.90/couple includes two nights lodging in the modern hotel, four cocktails per person in any of the hotel lounges, and a food credit of $19/person good in any of the casino's restaurants. Now that's a bargain! Availability of this package is irregular. See also page 186.

CONDOS ON THE LAKE:

Brockway Springs Resort, *P.O. Box 276, Kings Beach 95719, 916/546-4201; $395/week for one bedroom unit; private lakefront beach club and recreation center with saunas, boat dock, pool, children's wading pool, private beach, hot springs, and tennis courts.*

Carnelian Woods, *P.O. Box 62, Carnelian Bay 95711, 916/546-5924 (call collect for reservations); $245/week for one bedroom unit; one-mile parcourse, tennis courts, bicycles, scheduled social activities, access to lakefront beach club, recreation center with olympic-sized pool, jacuzzi, saunas, indoor and outdoor sports facilities.* Winter guests may enjoy an informal snow play area with saucers provided by the resort as well as use of a two-mile cross-country ski trail with necessary equipment provided by the resort.

Chinquapin, *P.O. Box RR, Tahoe City 95730, 916/583-6991; $450/week for a lakefront one-bedroom unit; private beach, tennis courts, pool, boating facilities.*

Coeur du Lac, *P.O. Box 4610, Incline Village, Nevada 89450, 702/831-3318; $300/week for one-bedroom unit; pool, jacuzzi, saunas, private beach 1½ blocks away.*

CONDOS FURTHER OUT:

Kingswood Village, *P.O. Box 1919, Kings Beach 95719, 916/546-2501 (call collect for reservations); $250/week for two-bedroom unit; pool, saunas, tennis courts, recreational game area, access to private beach club on the lake.*

Northstar, *P.O. Box 2499, Truckee 95734, 916/562-1111 (call collect for reservations); $225/week for one-bedroom unit; tennis courts, pool, par course, exercise room, saunas, whirlpool.* For an additional charge guests may use the facility's golf course, rent horses, send children (ages 4–12) to day camp, and join in special social events. (See photo next page.)

Tahoe Donner, *P.O. Drawer G, Truckee 95734, 916/587-2551 (reservations), 587-6028 (information); $110 and up/two nights; cribs, fireplaces, decks, kitchens, some washers and dryers, two-night minimum, golf course, tennis courts, beach club, dining facilities.* Located just

16 miles north of Lake Tahoe, Tahoe Donner is situated on Donner Lake and offers complete resort facilities. Ask about the special mid-week vacation package. Accommodations are condominiums and houses. Movies and social activities are scheduled each week, including special activities for young children and teenagers.

■ *WHERE TO EAT*

Cantina Los Tres Hombres, *8791 N. Lake Blvd., Kings Beach, 916/546-4052.* For description see page 154. **Taco City** (690 N. Lake Blvd., Tahoe City, 916/583-4304) is under the same management and offers a similar menu. It is open daily for breakfast, lunch and dinner.

Clementine's Kitchen and Tavern, *2255 W. Lake Blvd., Tahoe City, 916/583-3134; daily for lunch and dinner, weekends for brunch; highchairs, booster seats, children's portions; reservations suggested.* This cozy, casual restaurant features an unpretentious old-fashioned decor and tasty home cooking.

Granite Chief Restaurant, *take the Squaw Valley tram to the top, 916/583-6985; daily 11am-5pm.* The tram ride is $5 for adults and $2.50 for children 16 and under.

Lake House Pizza, *600 N. Lake Blvd., Tahoe City, 916/583-2222; daily 11am-11pm; booster seats.* A choice of sitting inside or out on the deck and a stunning view of the lake are reason enough for dining here. The bonus is that there is a choice of 22 kinds of pizza made with wholewheat crust. Assorted sandwiches, salads, and steaks as well as exceptionally good homemade potato chips are also available. **The Great American Omelette Company** (916/583-2225) is located upstairs and serves breakfast weekdays and a champagne brunch on the weekends.

The Pepper House, *8497 N. Lake Blvd., Kings Beach, 916/546-2833; M-Sat 11am-7pm, closed Sun.* Breakfast, hot and cold sandwiches, and the special "peppersteak sandwich" made with steak, tomatoes, onions, peppers, mushrooms, and cheese on a French roll are all available at this fast-food spot.

The Squirrel's Nest, *P.O. Box 206, Homewood 95718, 916/525-7944; daily in summer 11:30am-3:30pm; reservations advised.* Enjoy outdoor seating in a funky atmosphere while you dine on homemade soups, salads, sandwiches, and desserts. An interesting shop adjoins.

Sunnyside Resort, *1850 W. Lake Blvd., Sunnyside, 916/583-4226; daily from 8am in summer, closed M & Tu in winter; highchairs, children's portions; reservations suggested for dinner.* It's hard to beat a summer meal enjoyed outside on the huge deck at Sunnyside resort. Watching the sailboats on the lake while you dine on a tasty hamburger or French-fried zucchini is sublime. On Sunday afternoons diners often enjoy live jazz.

Tahoe City Bakery, *in the lighthouse center, Tahoe City, 916/583-3068; daily 7am-5pm.* Fresh donuts, cinnamon bread, and other bakery goods are available to enjoy on the premises or to take out.

Tomfoolerys, *640 N. Lake Blvd., Tahoe City, 916/583-5700; reservations* *essential.* This cozy lakeside restaurant specializes in fondue. Entrees and supporting courses are finger foods, so you will find no cutlery on the tables at this popular spot. Dinners include cheese fondue, fondue bourguignonne, fish fondue (dipped in tempura batter), as well as individual dinners of Cornish game hen, fresh fish, stewed shrimp (shrimp boiled in beer), and steak.

■ *WHAT TO DO*

BEST BEACHES:

William Kent Beach, *south of Tahoe City.* This is a small, rocky beach and parking is difficult. But it's worth it.

Sand Harbor Beach, *in Nevada south of Incline, $2/car.* This is a perfect beach. The sand is fine, lifeguards are on duty, and there is plenty of parking. Arrive early on weekends to assure getting in.

BIKING:

The Bike Shop, *255 N. Lake Blvd., Tahoe City, 916/583-4961; rentals available.*

Bike Trails begin in Tahoe City and follow the North Shore to Tahoe Pines.

Blyth Olympic Ice Arena, *see page 186.*

Boreal Alpine Slide, *off Hwy 80 at the Castle Peak exit, ten miles west of Truckee (P.O. Box 39, Truckee 95734), 916/426-3666; daily July–Sept 10am–10pm; adults $3, 7–11 $2, under 6 free, no children under age 2.* Imported from Germany, the Boreal slide is the only one of its kind in Northern California. Riders take a chair skilift to the top of the mountain and then sled 3,000 feet (more than ½ mile) down to the bottom. Riders can control their speed, so the ride down can be described as either exhilarating or relaxing.

Canoes, Jet Skis. Rentals are available at Common's Beach in Tahoe City.

Fishing Charters. The captain supplies bait and tackle. You supply a fishing license which may be purchased at most sporting goods shops in the area. The fee is approximately $30/person. Children are generally less. For further details call 916/546-4533, 583-4602, 583-6262.

MINIATURE GOLF:

Bobergs' Mini Golf, *Kings Beach.*

Ponderosa Ranch, *P.O. Box AP, Incline Village, Nevada 89450, 702/831-0691; daily June–Oct 10am–6pm, call for spring and fall schedule,*

closed in winter; adults $4, children $3. Created especially for film-
ing scenes for the TV show *Bonanza,* the Ponderosa Ranch is now
open to the public for tours. Visitors are given a bumpy ride from the
parking lot up the hill to the ranch, then a guided tour and talk on
the history and special features of the site. After the tour, you may
explore on your own and discover the petting farm and outdoor barbecue restaurant. The tin cups in which beer and soft drinks are
served make great souvenirs. Located adjacent is a stable where you
can take a ride over dusty trails and see some spectacular views of
the lake. A breakfast ride leaves daily at 8am. Call 702/831-2154
for reservations and information.

River Rafting/Inner Tubing, *begins on the Truckee River at the "Y"*
(where Hwys 89 and 28 intersect) in Tahoe City. It takes about
two hours to reach the River Ranch located four miles down-
river. Children must be at least four years old. It is first-come, first-
served, so get here before 11am if you want to avoid the crowds.
Summer hours are daily from 9:30am to 3:30pm. Prices are $7 per
person. Wear swimsuits and waterproof shoes. Raft rentals and transportation back may be arranged through:

Mountain Air Sports, *P.O. Box 1499, Tahoe City 95730, 916/583-
5606.*

Truckee River Raft Rentals, *P.O. Box 1618, Tahoe City 95730,
916/583-9724.*

This trip can also be made on an inner tube.

Truckee River Bridge or "Fanny Bridge," *junction of Hwys 89 and 28*
in Tahoe City. You'll know you're here when you see all the fannies
lined up. Spectators gather here to view the large trout that congregate beneath the bridge. This dam is the only outlet from the lake.

U.S. Forest Service Visitor Programs, *Wm. Kent Visitor Center, 916/
583-3642.*

Winter activities, *see page 185.*

SIDE TRIP:
RENO

Greater Reno Chamber of Commerce
P.O. Box 3499
(133 N. Sierra St.)
Reno, Nevada 89505
702/786-3030
Offers a reservation service.

MGM Grand, Reno.

Reno Reservation Service
702/786-5454
For packages only.

■ *CHILDCARE*

A Small World School, *4701 Neil Rd., Reno 89502, 702/825-2522;
open 24 hours; age 2 (must be toilet trained) to age 12; $1/hour, 4
hour minimum; reservations not necessary; state licensed.*

■ *WHERE TO EAT*

Big Yellow House Restaurant, *4990 S. Virginia, 702/827-3016; daily
from 5pm.* Though service is buffet-style, this restaurant is run along
the lines of the Old Santa Cruz Railway (see page 23).

Pizza Time Theatre, *in Greenbrae Shopping Center off Hwy 80, Sparks,
702/358-9228; highchairs, booster seats.* Children and parents alike
are sure to enjoy this new star in the family restaurant galaxy. The
menu consists of all the things kids love best: pizza, sandwiches, and
make-your-own sundaes. Adults may appreciate the fact that there
is also a salad bar as well as beer and wine. Entertainment is offered
in the form of computerized performances by the Pizza Time char-
acters and the latest in video, pinball and arcade games.

■ *WHAT TO DO*

CASINOS:

Circus Circus, *500 N. Sierra St., toll-free reservations 800/648-5010.* Here you can dine in any of three dining rooms (the 120 foot buffet serves inexpensive lunches and dinners) and enjoy free continuous circus acts which occur daily from 11am to midnight. Overnight lodging in this gaudy casino is quite reasonable—from $20 up.

MGM Grand, *2500 E. Second St., toll-free reservations 800/648-4585.* You could easily spend all day inside this gigantic, glittery casino which claims to be the world's largest. Inside there are seven restaurants (including an ice cream parlor), over 40 shops (including a candy shop with huge barrels of unusual candies and a photo shop where you can have your picture taken with a live lion), a bowling alley and pinball parlor, a jai alai court, two movie theaters, and a wedding chapel as well as plenty of slot machines. Guest staying at the hotel have access to a pool, tennis courts, and a health club.

Harrah's Auto Collection, *P.O. Box 10, Reno 89504, 702/786-3232 x370; daily 9am–6pm; adults $4, 13–20 $2, 5–12 $1.50, under 5 free.* Over 1,000 classic antique cars have been restored and fill three huge showrooms of this museum. The best way to get here is via one of the free shuttle buses (a double-decker bus and 1906 San Francisco cable car) which leave regularly from Harrah's casino.

FAMILY CAMPS

Remember the good old days when you were a kid and got to go away to summer camp? Bet you thought those days were gone for good. Well, they're not. Sponsored by city recreation departments, university alumni organizations, and private enterprise, family camps are alive and well and provide a reasonably-priced, organized vacation experience. All of these camps are open to anyone, members or non-members, with the exception of Stanford Sierra Camp which is open only to people with a Stanford affiliation.

Housing is sometimes in primitive tents or cabins (often without electricity or water) and bedding is usually provided by the campers. Unlike traditional camping, at a family camp you can look forward to a well-organized recreation program, meal service and clean-up, special programs for the children, an informal atmosphere where you'll easily make new friends, and no tents to pitch.

Family camps offer all or some of the following activities: river or pool swimming, hikes, fishing, volleyball, ping pong, badminton, hayrides, various tournaments, campfires, teen programs, craft programs, songfests, playgrounds, tennis, and horseback riding.

Detailed rate information, an itemization of facilities, season dates, and route directions can all be obtained from the camp reservation offices. Call or write for their free brochures.

Alumni Vacation Center, University of California Santa Barbara, *Santa Barbara 93106, 805/961-3123; weekly rates: adults and teenagers $210, 8–11 $155, 3–7 $145, 2 and under $85, discount for Alumni Club members; season: mid-June through mid-September; location: U.C. Santa Barbara campus; special facilities: dorm suite with daily maid service, eight hours of childcare (all ages) each day, tennis and swimming lessons, ten tennis courts, pool, organized social activities.*

Camp Concord, *Concord Department of Leisure Services, Civic Center, 2974 Salvio St., Concord 94519, 415/671-3270; daily rates: adults $15, 9–16 $12, 4–8 $9, under 4 free, rates higher for non-residents; season: July and August; location: near Camp Richardson at South Lake Tahoe.*

Camp Sierra, *Associated Cooperatives Inc., 4801 Central Ave., Richmond 94804, 415/526-0440; weekly rates: adults $82–$99, 5–11 $47.50, 1–4 $33.50, under 1 $12; season: two weeks in July; location: in a pine forest between Huntington and Shaver Lakes, about 65 miles east of Fresno; special facilities: craft programs for pre-schoolers, elementary, and pre-teens, special entertainment for teens, children's playground, choice of accommodations—camping, cabins, or duplexes.*

Cazadero Music Camp/Family Music Camp, *CAMPS Inc., 1744 University Ave., Berkeley 94703, 415/549-2396; weekly rates: 2 people/ $350, 3/$450, 4/$520, 5/$600, Berkeley residents get a 10% discount; season: one week in August; location: in the Russian River area; special facilities: day care for infants, program for children 2–6, recreation and crafts program, special music classes open to everyone regardless of ability or experience, choice of dormitories or platform tents.*

Emandal, *see page 70.*

Feather River Family Camp, *Office of Parks and Recreation, 1520 Lakeside Dr., Oakland 94612, 415/273-3896; daily rates: adults $14.60, 10–15 $11.60, 6–9 $8.60, 3–5 $6.40, 1–2 $3.40, under 1 free, rates higher for non-residents and for stays of less than four days; season: July and August; location: the Plumas National Forest, northeast of Quincy, a short drive from Lake Tahoe; special facilities: activities and play area for young children, special program for teens, special "theme weeks."*

Kennolyn's Family Camp, *8205 Glen Haven Rd., Soquel 95073, 408/ 475-1430; weekly rates: adults $185, 13–17 $175, 6–12 $140, 3–5 $80, 2 and under $55 (includes babysitting); season: last two weeks of summer; location: four miles from Soquel; special facilities: three tennis courts, pool, instruction in horseback riding, riflery, archery, gymnastics, crafts, sailing, and soccer, special children's programs, darkroom access for photographers.*

Lair of the Bear, *Lair Reservations, Alumni House, University of California, Berkeley 94720, 415/642-0221; weekly rates: adults $142, 13–17 $124, 5–12 $86, 2–4 $60, 6 months–1 $35, under 6 months free, non-members of the Alumni Club pay an additional $15 fee; season: mid-June through August; location: near Pinecrest in the Stanislaus National Forest; special facilities: choice of two camps*

(Camp Blue and Camp Gold), free swimming and tennis lessons, pool, three tennis courts, special program for children 6 and over, supervised play for children 2—7, babysitting can be arranged for an additional fee.

Mather Family Camp, *San Francisco Recreation and Park Department, McLaren Lodge, Golden Gate Park, San Francisco 94117, 415/ 558-4870; daily rates: adults $15, 11–17 $12, 6–10 $8, 2–5 $6, under 2 $1, rates higher for non-residents; season: mid-June through August; location: on the rim of the Tuolumne River gorge, near Yosemite National Park; special facilities: children's programs, pool; horseback riding for an additional fee.*

Montecito Sequoia Lodge, Family Camp Program, *1485 Redwood Dr., Los Altos 94022, 415/967-8612; location: in Sequoia National Forest; weekend rates: adults $88, children less, includes six meals and two nights lodging; season: all year (except mid-June to mid-August), full family camp program last two weeks of August only; special facilities, depending on season: sailing, canoeing, boating, lake and pool swimming, tennis, archery, riflery, photography darkroom, fishing; waterskiing and horseback riding are available for an additional fee.* Inquire about their special running camp. For winter activities see page 188.

San Jose Family Camp, *San Jose Parks and Recreation Department, 151 W. Mission St., room 203, San Jose 95110, 408/277-4000 x4661; daily rates: adults $18, 11–16 $15, 6–10 $10, 1–5 $7, under 1 free, rates higher for non-residents and for stays of less than three days; season: June through August; location: middle fork of the Tuolumne River in the Stanislaus National Forest, about 16 miles from Groveland and 30 miles from Yosemite National Park.*

Skylake Yosemite Camp, *summer: P.O. Box 25, Wishon 93669, 209/ 642-3720; rest of year: P.O. Box 11163, Palo Alto 94306, 415/ 493-4075; weekly rates: adults and teenagers $115, 7–12 $95, 3–6 $63.75, 2 and under $32.50; season: one week in June, two weeks in August; location: on Bass Lake, 20 miles from Yosemite National Park; special facilities: two tennis courts, canoes, sailboats; waterskiing and horseback riding available for an additional fee; no special children's programs.*

Stanford Sierra Camp, *Stanford Alumni Association, Bowman Alumni House, Stanford 94305, 415/497-2021; weekly rates: adults $235, 5–11 $175, 3–4 $120, under 3 $50; actual rates depend on type of accommodations and number of people; must be a member of Stanford Alumni Association; season: mid-June through August;*

location: Fallen Leaf Lake, about 15 miles from South Lake Tahoe; special facilities: recreation programs for children 3 and over, baby-sitting for a fee, instruction and equipment for waterskiing and aquaplaning, two tennis courts, movies.

Tuolumne Family Camp, *Berkeley Camps Office, 2180 Milvia St., Berkeley 94704, 415/644-6520; daily rates: adults $15, 1–14 $11, under 1 free, rates higher for non-residents and for stays of less than three days; season: mid-June through August; location: south fork of the Tuolumne River, a few miles from Yosemite National Park.*

HOUSEBOATS

Living in a houseboat for a few days is an unusual way to get away from it all. Put on your swimsuit and dive off your boat to enjoy a refreshing swim. Fish for your dinner while you sunbathe. Dock in a sheltered, quiet cove for the night.

Houseboats are equipped with kitchens and flush toilets. Most rental agencies require that you bring your own bedding, linens and groceries. Almost everything else will already be on your floating hotel—including lifejackets.

Rates vary quite a bit depending on the time of year and how many people are in your party. A group of six to ten people gets the best rates. Rates range from $300 to $950/week depending on the size of the boat—about $500 for a medium-sized boat. Contact rental facilities directly for their specifications and rates. Weekend rentals are usually available only in the off-season; in the summer minimum rentals are usually one week.

LAKE OROVILLE

Lime Saddle Marina, *Pentz Rd. Oroville, 916/534-6950.*
For more information on this area contact:
Oroville Chamber of Commerce
1789 Montgomery
Oroville 95965
916/533-2542

LAKE SHASTA

Bridge Bay Resort & Marina, *10300 Bridge Bay Rd., Redding 96001,* 916/275-3021

Holiday Flotels, *P.O. Box 336, Redding 96099, 916/246-1283.*

Holiday Harbor, *P.O. Box 112, O'Brien 96070, 916/238-2412.*

Margus Houseboats, *P.O. Box 599, Redding 96099, 916/243-4353.*

Silverthorn Bay Resort, *P.O. Box 419, Redding 96099, 916/275-2332.*

For more information on houseboating on Lake Shasta contact:
Shasta-Cascade Wonderland Association
P.O. Box 1988
Redding 96099
916/243-2643

SACRAMENTO DELTA

Herman & Helen's Marina, *Venice Island Ferry, Stockton 95209, 209/951-4634.* If you have an R.V., inquire about their "camp-a-float" apparatus.

Holiday Flotels, *11540 W. Eight Mile Rd., Stockton 95209, 209/477-9544.*

Paradise Point Marina, *8095 Rio Blanco Rd., Stockton 95209, 209/952-1000.*

For more information on houseboating on the Delta contact:
Stockton Chamber of Commerce
1105 N. El Dorado
Stockton 95202
209/466-7066

Rio Vista Chamber of Commerce
60 Main St.
Rio Vista 94571
707/374-2700

RIVER TRIPS

The adventure of rafting down a changing and unpredictable river offers a real escape for the harried, city-weary participant. But don't expect it to be relaxing. Participants are expected to help with setting up and breaking camp and are sometimes mercilessly exposed to the elements. While not dangerous when done with experienced guides, an element of risk is involved. Still, most participants walk away ecstatic and addicted to the experience.

The outfitter will provide shelter, food, and equipment for the trip. You need only bring your sleeping gear and personal items. Costs range from $87 to $165/person for an overnight run. Some one-day trips are available. Seasons and rivers vary with each company. The minimum age for children ranges from 6 to 10. For details contact the tour operators.

American River Touring Association, *1307 Harrison St., Oakland 94612, 415/465-9355.*

ECHO: The Wilderness Company Inc., *6505 Telegraph Ave., Oakland 94609, 415/658-5075, 658-5080.*

Whitewater Voyages/River Exploration Ltd., *P.O. Box 906, El Sobrante 94530, 415/222-5994.*

Wilderness Adventures, *430 Buckeye Terrace #3, Redding 96001, 916/243-3091.*

PACK TRIPS

Packing your equipment onto horses or mules allows for a much easier and luxurious trek into the wilderness than does backpacking. All necessary equipment, food, and paraphernalia can be packed onto these beasts of burden. You need simply make the choice of the type of pack trip you desire.

On a *spot pack trip* the packers will load the animals with your gear, take them to your prearranged campsite, unload your gear, and return to the pack station with the pack animals. They will return to repack your gear on the day you are to leave. You may either hike or ride on horses to your campsite. If you ride, you will usually have a choice of keeping the horses at your campsite or of having the packers take them back out. If you wish to keep them, you will need to arrange in advance for a corral and feed, and you should be experienced with horses. Do not bring along small children who haven't had at least basic riding instruction. A more rugged trip (where you move your campsite each day) or an easier trip (with all expenses and a guide included) can usually be arranged with the packer.

Prices will vary according to which of these options you choose. For example: guided trips $40–$55/day, drop pack trips $200/7–10 days. Seasons are usually limited to the summer and most have special rates for children. Children must generally be at least five years old. For detailed information contact any of the following packers:

McGee Creek Pack Station, *Box 1054, Bishop 93514, 714/935-4324 (Sept–May 714/873-4350); location: John Muir Wilderness.*

Rainbow Pack Outfit, *R.R. 1, Box 26, Bishop 93514, 714/873-4485 (Sept 15–June 15, 719 Springfield Ave., Ventura 93003, 805/647-5351); location: Inyo National Forest and Kings Canyon National Park.*

Red's Meadow Pack Station, *P.O. Box 395, Mammoth Lakes 93546, 714/934-2345 (Oct–June 714/873-3928); location: Yosemite and Sequoia National Parks, John Muir and Minaret Wildernesses.*

Rock Creek Pack Station, *Box 248, Bishop 93514, 714/935-4493 (Oct–June 714/872-8331); location: Yosemite and Sequoia National Parks and John Muir Wilderness.*

For general information and a list of more packers contact:

Eastern High Sierra Packers Association, *P.O. Box 147, Bishop 93514, 714/873-8405*

High Sierra Packers Association, *Western Unit, P.O. Box 123, Madera 93639.*

Now llamas too, are available for guided pack trips. They're used to this chore; they've been doing it for over 2,000 years in the Andes. And they are so gentle even a four-year-old can lead them. For details contact the following outfitters:

Mama's Llamas, *P.O. Box 655, El Dorado 95623, 916/622-2566.*

Shasta Llamas, *P.O. Box 5160, Oakland 94605, 415/635-0286 and P.O. Box 1137, Mt. Shasta 96067, 916/926-3959.*

WINTER SNOW FUN

The number of ski areas is overwhelming. I have listed only ones which are primarily family-oriented. Rates vary quite a bit (for example all-day lift tickets range from $6 to $16 and childcare ranges from 75¢ to $2/hour), so always call ahead for prices and other information. Be sure to inquire about midweek packages; when available, they can save you considerable money. The least crowded times at the resorts are after Thanksgiving, the first two weeks in January, and late in the season.

CROSS-COUNTRY SKIING

Cross-country skiing is becoming more popular each year. Some of the reasons for this surging popularity are the advantages it has over downhill skiing: there are no lift tickets to purchase; the equipment needed is less expensive; it is considered to be safer; it can be enjoyed in groups; and it allows you to get away from crowds. But it also requires more stamina and is less exhilarating.

Many specialized centers offer equipment rentals, lessons, and maintained trails. Some also offer lodging, special guided tours, the option of downhill facilities, and reduced rates for children. Children age 4 and up are usually taught in classes with their parents. Some centers have "children only" classes.

If you have the strength, you can carry a small child in a backpack.

It is a good idea for beginners to rent equipment and take a few lessons (lessons average $6 to $10) to learn safety guidelines and basic skiing techniques. Once the basics are learned, you can practice this sport just about anywhere there's a foot of snow. All centers will let skiers use their maintained trails for a small fee.

SNOW PLAY

Toboggans, saucers, inner tubes, and sometimes sleds are the equipment found in snow play areas. They are inexpensive to buy but bulky to store. Many commercial areas will let you use your own equipment, but some require that you rent their equipment.

This section also includes information about ice skating, snowcat rides, snowshoe walks, and miscellaneous other winter facilities.

NORTH

Lassen Park Ski Area, *Lassen Volcanic National Park, Mineral 96063, 916/595-3306, 595-3376; location: 90 miles north of Chico; downhill and cross-country; lodging nearby, Childs Meadows Resort 916/ 595-4411, 595-3391, packages available; free beginning ski lessons, free snowshoe walks and free use of snowshoes each weekend (916/ 595-4444), free snow play area.* This is California's "undiscovered national park." The natural phenomena here (hot steam vents, mud pots, etc.) make for a quite unusual and interesting ski tour.

SOUTH LAKE TAHOE

Heavenly Valley, *Box A-T, South Lake Tahoe 95705, 916/541-1330, toll-free 800/648-5450; location: South Lake Tahoe; downhill only; lodging nearby; childcare in town (see page 152), children's ski school (5-12), private classes for younger children.* This is America's largest ski area. It offers skiing in two states.

Kirkwood Meadows, *Box 1, Kirkwood 95646, 209/258-6000; location: 30 miles south of Lake Tahoe on Hwy 88; downhill only; lodging: Kirkwood Condominiums (contact above phone) and Kays Resort (cabins), Kirkwood Star Route, Pioneer 95666, 209/258-8598; childcare center (3-8), children's ski school (4-7).*

Kirkwood Ski Touring Center, *P.O. Box 77, Kirkwood 95646, 209/258-8864; cross-country only.*

Sugar House West, *P.O. Box 8135, South Lake Tahoe 95731, 916/541-6811; location: off Hwy 50 at Yank's Station; cross-country only; lodging nearby, packages available.*

Sundown, *Box 54, Kirkwood 95646, 209/258-8543; location: off Hwy 88 twelve miles east of Kirkwood; downhill only; lodging on premises; childcare available, children's ski school (3-7).*

■ *SNOW PLAY*

Busy Bee Hill, *1360 Ski Run Blvd. (P.O. Box 316), South Lake Tahoe 95705, 916/544-3361; weekends only.* Use of snow play area is free, but you must rent their toboggans and saucers ($3-$6). There is a mechanical toboggan return.

ICE SKATING:

Ski Run Ice Arena, *900 Ski Run Blvd. (P.O. Box 14272), South Lake Tahoe 95705, 916/541-6883; open daily; adults $3, 3-13 $2, 2 and under free, skate rental $1.25.* This is an outdoor arena with a great view of the lake.

Tahoe Keys Marina, *located at east end of Venice Blvd. next to Upper Truckee River (P.O. Box 1239); daily Nov–Feb, 6–10pm; skating free, skate rentals available.*

Sleigh Rides, *leave across from the Sahara Tahoe casino and at Stateline Stables (916/541-9896); daily; adults $4, children $3.50, special family rates.*

Snowshoe Walks, *Lake Tahoe Visitor's Center, 916/525-7232, 544-6420.* Call for schedule. Bring your own snowshoes.

Winter Wonderland, *3672 Verdon (P.O. Box 387), South Lake Tahoe 95705, 916/544-7903; daily; $2.* This is a snow play area.

NORTH LAKE TAHOE

Alpine Meadows, *P.O. Box AM, Tahoe City 95730, 916/583-4232 (for reservations call 916/583-1045 collect); location: six miles northwest of Tahoe City; downhill and cross-country; lodging nearby, packages available; childcare center "snow school" (3-6), children's ski school (6-12).* Alpine Meadows has the longest ski season at Lake Tahoe. Ask about their five day "learn to ski" program.

Boreal, *P.O. Box 39, Truckee 95734, 916/426-3666; location: Castle Peak exit off Hwy 80 ten miles west of Truckee; downhill only; lodging on premises, packages available; children's ski school (4-8).* Boreal offers night skiing daily until 10pm. You may want to take advantage of their offer of a free hour of skiing. Each morning between 9 and 10am, skiers may test their slopes at no charge.

Donner Ski Ranch, *P.O. Box 66, Norden 95724, 916/426-3578; location: on Hwy 40, 3½ miles off Hwy 80 at the Norden/Soda Springs exit; downhill and cross-country; lodging on premises, packages available.*

Homewood, *Box 165, Homewood 95718, 916/525-7256; location: six miles south of Tahoe City on Hwy 89; downhill only; lodging nearby; children's ski school (3-8), snow play area.*

Northstar, *P.O. Box 2499, Truckee 95734, 916/562-1111, call collect for reservations; location: off Hwy 267 between Truckee and Kings Beach; downhill and cross-country; lodging on premises (see page 161), packages available; children's ski school (6-12).* Lift tickets are limited to assure that the slopes don't get overcrowded. Special activities are scheduled each week.

Royal Gorge Nordic Ski Resort, *Donner Pass Rd (P.O. Box 178), Soda Springs 95728, 916/426-3793; location: near Donner Pass, at the Soda Springs/Norden exit of Hwy 80; cross-country only; lodging on premises, packages available; children's ski school (3-10).* Modeled after Scandinavian ski resorts, Royal Gorge offers the crème de la crème of Nordic skiing accommodations. A weekend includes two nights' lodging, transportation from the parking lot to the lodge by snowcat-drawn sleigh, five French meals, two days' trail passes, four half-day lessons, two seminars, access to a hot tub and sauna, night skiing, and the children's ski school!

Squaw Valley, *P.O. Box 2393, Olympic Valley 95730, 916/583-0121; location: seven miles north of Tahoe City off Hwy 89; lodging on premises, packages available; downhill and cross-country; childcare center (2-6), children's ski school (5-14), ice skating, snowcat rentals.* At Squaw Valley children under 12 ski free with their parents.

Tahoe Donner, *P.O. Drawer G, Truckee 95734, 916/587-6046, 587-9821; location: on Hwy 40, ½ mile from Hwy 80's Truckee/Donner Lake exit; downhill and cross-country; lodging on premises (see page 161); children's ski school (6 and up), snow play area.* Special cross-country programs occur each week: ski with Santa, morning nature tour, sauna tour, annual Donner Trail tour.

Tahoe Nordic Ski Center, *Box 1632, Tahoe City 95730, 916/583-9858; location: in Tahoe City; cross-country only; lodging nearby, packages available.*

Tahoe Ski Bowl, *Box 305, Homewood 95718, 916/525-5224, 525-5216; location: seven miles south of Tahoe City on Hwy 89; downhill only; lodging nearby; childcare center (3 and older), children's ski school (3 and older).*

▪ SNOW PLAY

Blyth Olympic Ice Arena, *Squaw Valley, 916/583-4211; Tu–F 1-3, 8-10pm, weekends 10am-3pm, 8-10pm; adults $2.50, 12 and under $2, skate rental 75¢.* This huge building was especially constructed for the 1960 winter olympic games. A skating school operates in the summer (916/583-1617).

Carnelian Woods Condominiums, *see page 161.*

Hyatt Lake Tahoe, *see page 161.* The Hyatt offers a children's "learn to ski" program for ages 5-12. Hours are 9am-5pm, and equipment and lunch are included.

North Lake Tahoe Regional Park, *at the end of National Ave. off Hwy 28 in Tahoe Vista, 916/546-2527, 702/831-3666; daily; free.* This is a snow play area for toboggans and saucers. Equipment and snowcat rentals are available only on weekends.

Powder Bowl Snow Play Area, *seven miles south of Tahoe City at entrance to Alpine Meadows (P.O. Box 5487), Tahoe City 95730, 916/583-4373; $3/person, includes use of equipment (saucers, inner tubes, mats).*

EAST

Bear Valley, *Box 8, Bear Valley 95223, 209/753-2301, cross-country 209/753-2844; location: on Hwy 4, 55 miles east of Angels Camp; downhill and cross-country; lodging on premises, packages available 209/753-2311; childcare center, children's ski school (6 and under).*

Dodge Ridge, *Box 1188, Pinecrest 95364, 209/965-3474; location: 30 miles east of Sonora off Hwy 108; downhill only; lodging nearby; childcare center (2–8).* This is considered to be one of the least expensive ski resorts.

Mt. Reba, *Box 38, Bear Valley 95223, 209/753-2301; lodging nearby; childcare center (3–8).*

■ *SNOW PLAY*

Bear River Lake Resort, *Hwy 88, Pioneer 95666, 209/295-4868; daily; $5/person for roundtrip ride by snowcat to an otherwise inaccessible spot, saucers only, saucer rentals and snowcat rentals; reservations essential.*

Calaveras Big Trees State Park, *see page 130.* Bring your own snowshoes for the ranger-led walks. Call for schedule 209/795-1181.

Cottage Springs, *eight miles east of Arnold on Hwy 4 (P.O. Box 215), Avery 95224, 209/795-1401, 795-1209; weekends; must rent their equipment, tubes only.*

Leland Meadows, *36 miles east of Sonora off Hwy 108 (P.O. Box 1498), Pinecrest 95364, 209/965-3745; daily; $3/person, under 5 free; rentals available; toboggans, saucers, tubes; snowcat tours and rentals and sleigh rides.* If you spend the night in one of the resort's townhouses, there is no charge to use the snow play area.

Little Sweden, *25 miles from Sonora on Hwy 108 (P.O. Box 281), Long Barn 95335, 209/586-2961; daily; $2/person; rentals available; toboggans, saucers, tubes.*

Long Barn Lodge Ice Rink, *23 miles east from Sonora off Hwy 108 (P.O. Box 100), Long Barn 95335, 209/586-3533; W–M 1–3:30 & 7:30–10pm; adults $3.25, 15 and under $2.50, skate rental $2.25/ $1.75.* The top of this rink is covered, but three sides are left open.

SOUTH/NATIONAL PARKS

Badger Pass Ski Area, *Yosemite National Park (see page 111), 209/372-4691, cross-country 209/372-4611 x244 (located in Curry Village); downhill and cross-country; lodging nearby, packages available (the "midweek ski special" is a bargain for families and includes childcare at no charge); childcare center (3 and over), children's ski school (4–6), snow play area.* This is California's oldest organized ski area. Cross-country is available through the Mountaineering School.

Mammoth Ski Touring Center, *P.O. Box 102, Mammoth Lakes 93546, 714/934-6955; location: off Hwy 203 50 miles north of Bishop; cross-country only; lodging nearby.*

Montecito Sequoia Nordic Ski Center, *Box 22, Grant Grove, Kings Canyon National Park 93633, reservations: 1485 Redwood Dr., Los Altos 94022, 415/967-8612; location: on Hwy 180 near Kings Canyon National Park; cross-country only; lodging on premises, packages*

available; ice skating. See also page 172.

Sequoia Ski Touring, *Sequoia National Park (see page 117), 209/565-3373; cross-country only; lodging nearby.*

■ *SNOW PLAY*

Sequoia/Kings Canyon, *see page 117, 209/565-3341.* **Snow play areas** are near Wolverton Ski Bowl (saucer rentals available on weekends), Lodgepole Visitor Center, and Azalea Campground in Grant Grove. Free use of **snowshoes** is available on the ranger-led walks here. Call 209/372-4461 for schedule and reservations.

Yosemite, *see page 111.* **Ice skating** may be enjoyed at the scenic outdoor rink located at Curry Village. Call 209/372-4611 x442 for daily schedule (adults $2, under 12 $1.50, skate rentals 75¢). Lessons are available. **Snowcat rides** operate from 9:30am–3:30pm daily at Badger Pass. For $2.50 riders get a one-hour sightseeing tour from inside a World War II army Weasel. For reservations call 209/373-4171.

A **snowplay area** is available at Badger Pass. Sleds, saucers, and toboggans are used. Saucers may be rented for $1.50. Another area is at Crane Flat near the Mariposa Grove just inside the south entrance. And yet another area may be reached by the Yosemite Mountain-Sugar Pine Railroad. Rentals are available. Call 209/683-5424 for details. Free ranger-led **snowshoe walks** leave from Badger Pass. For schedule call 209/372-4461 x32. Snowshoes may be rented for $4/day. A good place to snowshoe on your own is the Sequoia Forest Trail in Mariposa Grove.

CAMPING
REFERENCES

Because there are excellent resources available for information on campgrounds, I have mentioned only a few unusual campgrounds which otherwise might be missed. For more complete information, you will want to consult the following references: *California-Nevada Camping* and *Camping, California—North* (available free to California State Automobile Association

members). These booklets list camping fees and facilities.

The California State Park System (available by mail for $1: Department of Parks and Recreation, P.O. Box 2390, Sacramento 95811). This informative brochure contains a map which pinpoints all state parks, reserves, recreation areas, historic parks, and campgrounds. If you will be visiting numerous national parks and monuments, also ask for the brochure on the *Golden Eagle Passport.*

Western Campsites (a Sunset Book, Lane Publishing Co., $4.95). Updated annually, this is the *complete* camping guide. Everything you need to know is here.

TICKETRON CAMPSITE RESERVATIONS

Reservations are necessary at most state park campgrounds and can be made through Ticketron for a fee. This may be done in person (bring cash) or by mail. Reservations may be made as early as eight weeks in advance. For the Ticketron outlet located nearest you call 415/495-4089. For further information contact: Ticketron, P.O. Box 26430, San Francisco 94125, 415/393-6914.

ABOUT THE AUTHOR

Carole Terwilliger Meyers, a native San Franciscan, holds a B.A. degree in anthropology from San Francisco State University and an elementary teaching credential from Fresno State College. For five years she was the editor of the *San Francisco Bay Area ASPO* (Lamaze Natural Childbirth) *Newsletter;* for two years she wrote a travel column, "Getaways," for the *San Jose Mercury News.* Her articles have been published in *California Living, San Francisco Magazine,* and *New West* as well as numerous other magazines and newspapers. She resides in Berkeley with her husband and two children.

If you find yourself resembling Ebenezer Scrooge when the holiday season rolls around, this Bay Area guide book will help you get rid of the "bah humbugs." Packed with over 70 ideas on how to make the Christmas season special, this helpful book covers the gamut from finding the makings for a gingerbread house, to indulging in a traditional Christmas feast a la Washington Irving, to singing carols on a paddlewheel boat. There is even a special section on what to do with the kids when they get restless during the BIG WAIT. This comprehensive guide to Bay Area Christmas events is sure to get you *IN THE SPIRIT* and divest you of the holiday humbugs.

GETTING IN THE SPIRIT

Annual Bay Area Christmas Events

Carole Terwilliger Meyers

EATING OUT WITH THE KIDS IN SAN FRANCISCO AND THE BAY AREA

Carole Terwilliger Meyers

This unique guide helps make dining out as a family an enjoyable experience. It allows parents to choose restaurants which are equipped to accommodate their children. Parents will not find the usual hamburger, taco, and pizza chains listed. Instead they will find a variety of more unusual restaurants—all amenable to families. Each restaurant's description specifies the availability of highchairs and booster seats, average waiting time, and parking facilities—plus other important dining information.

HOW TO ORGANIZE A BABYSITTING COOPERATIVE

and Get Some <u>Free</u> Time Away From the Kids

by Carole Terwilliger Meyers

An essential and valuable resource book for anyone who is having trouble finding or paying for baby-sitters, this book explains in detail every aspect of setting up a baby-sitting cooperative. Chapter titles include "Ways to Recruit Members," "Choosing Rules," "Book-keeping Methods," and "Using the Co-op for Fun." Co-ops which are already established will also find the information included to be helpful. With the aid of this book, parents need no longer be constantly on the lookout for new babysitters nor need they go through the unnerving process of testing their reliability.

ORDER FORM

_____ How to Organize a Babysitting Cooperative, hardcover @ $8.95 each . . . $_____

_____ How to Organize a Babysitting Cooperative, soft cover @ $3.95 each . . . $_____

_____ Eating Out With the Kids in San Francisco and the Bay Area @ $4.95 each . $_____

_____ Weekend Adventures for City-Weary Families @ $5.95 each . . . . $_____

_____ Getting In the Spirit, Annual Bay Area Christmas Events @ $2.50 each. . $_____

subtotal $_____

☐ Please send fund-raising brochure   6½% sales tax (Calif. residents only) $_____

☐ Please send retailer's brochure   postage/handling $_____.75

total amount enclosed $_____

SEND TO (please print):

name_____ phone_____

address_____

city,state,zip_____

ALL ORDERS MUST BE PREPAID. Make check or money order payable to CAROUSEL PRESS and mail to: **CAROUSEL PRESS**, P.O. Box 6061, Albany, CA 94706